UNIVERSAL FLY TYING GUIDE

DICK STEWART

cover: Silver Doctor

published by
Mountain Pond Publishing
Box 797
North Conway, New Hampshire 03860

distributed by:
Universal Vise Corporation
16 Union Avenue
Westfield, Massachusetts 01086
and
The Countryman Press, Inc.
Box 175
Woodstock, Vermont 05091

CONTENTS

Other books by Dick Stewart
    Fly Tying Tips
    The Hook Book
    Bass Flies
    Trolling Flies for Trout & Salmon (with Bob Leeman)
    Flies for Atlantic Salmon (with Farrow Allen)
    Flies for Steelhead (with Farrow Allen)
    Flies for Bass & Panfish (with Farrow Allen)
    Flies for Saltwater (with Farrow Allen)
    Flies for Trout (with Farrow Allen)

Published by:
    Mountain Pond Publishing Corp.
    P.O. Box 797
    North Conway, NH 03860

ISBN: 0-936644-20-6
© Copyright 1979, April 1994 by Richard B. Stewart
Printed in the United States of America
Second edition, first printing

Atlantic salmon flies supplied by Hunter's Angling Supplies, New Boston, NH
Steelhead flies supplied by Blue Heron Fly Shop, Idleyld Park, OR

INTRODUCTION

While the motivation to start fly tying may stem from different factors, many people find that it develops into a full hobby unto itself. Perhaps the appeal is the opportunity to keep the hands and imagination busy on cold winter evenings. In recent years we have learned a great deal about entomology as it relates to fishing. While many trout are still caught with flies and methods developed long ago, fishermen are finding that more sophisticated flies and techniques are often required today. Local tackle shops are often unable to supply adequate flies, and this might germinate a desire to tie your own.

Any angler who learns to tie his own flies will discover that the new knowledge gained will carry forth to improve streamside results. It is hoped that this book might serve to assist both beginning and more advanced tiers who are interested in acquiring such knowledge. For beginners, the following advice cannot be over-emphasized:

TAKE LESSONS, whether individual or through fly-tying courses offered locally. Competent instruction is far more worthwhile than trial and error methods. You might also consider buying or renting some of the new instructional videotapes - they can be quite enlightening.

USE GOOD MATERIALS. Tiers like to compare their flies against professionally tied samples and may find the results disappointing. Often the principal difference is the quality of the materials used. No amount of skill can compensate for poor materials.

OBSERVE each detail of properly tied flies. These flies have been designed in minute detail for maximum success. Pay particular attention to all proportions.

PRACTICE to develop skills and gain familiarity with materials. Each feather or fur has different characteristics which can only be learned through continued handling.

CONSTRUCTION TIPS: DURABILITY - is achieved primarily by keeping good tension on the thread throughout the tying procedure. The application of cements, while useful, is no substitute for proper thread tension. SPARSENESS - a common error is the excess use of material, thus overdressing the fly. Generally, it's better to use too little material than too much. SIZE - is the most important factor in a fly. Having fewer patterns in a wide range of recommended sizes is better than to have many patterns all tied on the same size hooks. PATTERNS - a variety of relatively easy, yet effective flies which a beginning trout fisherman might start with are:

Adams	Brown Bivisible	Hares Ear Nymph	Serendipity
Black Flying Ant	Gray Hackle	Foam Hopper	Woolly Bugger
Black Nose Dace	Elk Hair Caddis	Mickey Finn	Zug Bug

Catching fish on home-tied flies adds a new level of satisfaction to the total fly-fishing experience. This often leads to learning more about nature's realm and a greater appreciation of our environment. Your respectfulness toward our common woods, water and wildlife is appreciated by your fellow anglers.

BASIC TOOLS

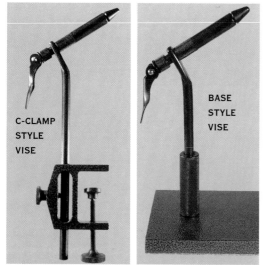

C-CLAMP STYLE VISE

BASE STYLE VISE

VISE The most important, and probably most expensive tool used in fly tying is the vise. Its primary function is to hold the hook securely. It may be held in position with a C-clamp affixed to a table edge, or else it will feature a heavily weighted base which can be placed upon any flat surface. Most vises are stationary models which remain in one position, although they might have several possible adjustments. A second type, called a rotary vise, serves a dual function since it can be used as a stationary model but is also designed to rotate the hook to assist in the winding of materials. Many models are available at a wide range of prices; however, the least expensive models will usually prove inadequate. Features to look for include the ability to hold a wide range of hook sizes, smoothness of the finish, height adjustments, and ease of operation.

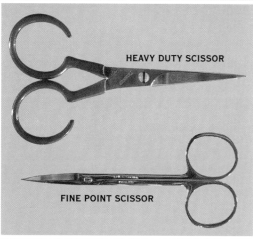

HEAVY DUTY SCISSOR

FINE POINT SCISSOR

SCISSORS Small very sharp scissors with narrow fine points are indispensable for the detailed work of fly tying. Large finger holes are preferred by experienced tiers, who keep the scissors on their fingers throughout the tying procedure. Heavier scissors are used on coarse materials primarily to preserve the points and sharpness of the fine pair. Serrated blades on heavier scissors help prevent materials from slipping away as they are being cut. Most fly tying material suppliers offer scissors specially designed for this purpose. In some cases where the tips are too thick, the points can be carefully filed down from the outside. Both straight and curved blades are available with the choice being primarily a matter of personal preference.

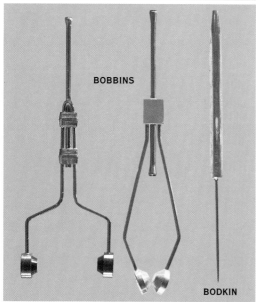

BOBBINS

BODKIN

BOBBIN This is a tool which holds the spool of thread during the tying operation. The bobbin permits very accurate control over both the placement of each individual thread winding on the hook, and the very important thread tension which is the basis of building a strong, durable fly. Also the bobbin provides sufficient weight to prevent unravelling of thread when the hands must be free for other purposes. Modern ceramic-tube bobbins eliminate the sharp edges often associated with metal-tube bobbins.

BODKIN A simple, inexpensive device consisting of a needle inserted into a handle for the sake of convenience. It is used for a great many operations such as applying head cement, picking out stray fibers, cleaning out the eye of a hook, separating fibers, and picking out dubbing fur. Some bodkins have a magnet built within to pick up hooks, others incorporate a half hitch tool as the handle.

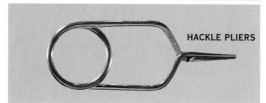

HACKLE PLIERS

HACKLE PLIERS These are used to grip hackle feathers by the tips and to hold them securely as they are wound around or applied to the fly. They must have a firm grip as hackles are often very small and will slip out of the jaws quite easily. Sharp edges on the pliers will cut the feather and should be avoided. Low quality hackle pliers can be most exasperating.

Many tools have been designed to assist fly tiers with specific procedures. Some of the most useful include: HALF HITCH TOOL, with a hole in each end is used to make half hitch knots at the head of the fly, particularly useful on Muddler Minnows; BOBBIN THREADER, very inexpensive but saves on patience when trying to get thread through the bobbin tube, especially once it becomes clogged with wax; TWEEZERS, very useful for picking up small hooks and for other occasions when you need to pick out very small feathers or fibers; WHIP FINISHER, a tool that requires practice to use properly, but once mastered, enables one to rapidly tie a whip finish knot, the most secure manner to tie off your thread upon completion of a fly; HAIR STACKER, essentially a tube into which bucktail or other hair is inserted, tips downward, then tapped against desk or table to evenly align the hair tips when used for wings or tails.

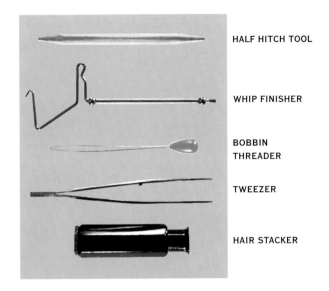

HALF HITCH TOOL

WHIP FINISHER

BOBBIN THREADER

TWEEZER

HAIR STACKER

HOOKS

A hook is the most basic ingredient of a fly and has recently been appropriately described as the "backbone" of any fly. A wide variety of hooks are manufactured specifically for tying flies with quality products coming from Norway, England and Japan. Various sizes of fly tying hooks are offered ranging from a designation of #1 to #28, with the highest number representing the smallest hook. Additionally, even larger hooks have size designations from #1/0 to #6/0 with higher numbers being larger hooks. The sizes most commonly used for trout flies range from #6 to #16, although there is good occasion to use either larger or smaller hooks, particularly the latter. In addition to size, another specification is hook length, as shown in the accompanying chart which pictures hooks of the same size but with varied shank lengths. A stubby beetle imitation cannot be properly tied on a very long hook, and, conversely, a long slim minnow imitation requires the use of a longer shank. Hook wire weight is another consideration since a heavy wire is stronger and also helps a fly to sink. Light wire helps reduce the tendency to sink, is generally preferred for floating flies, and its smaller diameter offers less resistance to hook penetration. The most common hook eye type is turned down using tapered wire. A straight eye or turned up eye may be used to maximize the point clearance on very small flies, and these eye types are also used to achieve special effects on some flies. The most basic hook shapes are illustrated, with there being little consensus as to which is best. Fly tying hooks generally have a straight bend, i.e. the point is not offset to one side. Hooks can be converted to barbless or semi-barbed by carefully crimping down the barb with flat nose pliers. This seems to help hook penetration with no loss of holding ability. Another worthwhile practice is to sharpen all hooks before beginning to tie. Other styles such as keel, flybody, Swedish, nymph form, parachute, and popper hooks are also available and worthy of attention and experimentation. For more information see the Hook Equivalence Chart on page 11.

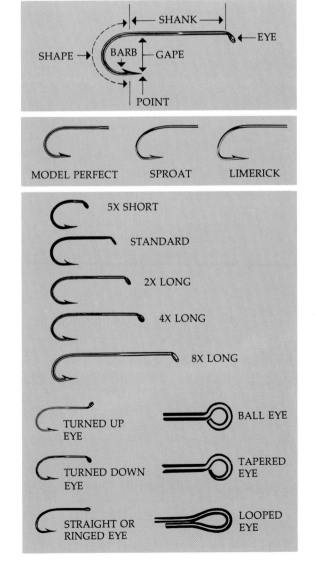

SHANK

EYE

SHAPE →

BARB — GAPE

POINT

MODEL PERFECT   SPROAT   LIMERICK

5X SHORT

STANDARD

2X LONG

4X LONG

8X LONG

TURNED UP EYE

BALL EYE

TURNED DOWN EYE

TAPERED EYE

STRAIGHT OR RINGED EYE

LOOPED EYE

MATERIALS

The materials described here represent those most commonly used in fly tying. Many are available through a great variety of sources, others must be purchased from specialized fly-tying materials suppliers. While these are the traditional and tested materials, one should not hesitate to experiment with other materials for this is how innovations in fly tying come about. If you don't have some of the materials required, substitution is quite acceptable for your personal flies; however, be certain the replacement material has characteristics similar to the original material specified.

THREAD—Fly tying thread is made of either twisted (round) or untwisted (flat) fibers. At one time silk was commonly used but today nylon, polyester or kevlar are favored. Nylon is most available, is quite strong, but does stretch slightly. Thread diameter is designated by numbers beginning with 1/0 through the smaller 8/0. Larger threads progress from size "A" through the larger size "E". Small threads build up less bulk and weight than large threads, but are not as strong. Nylon threads are now commonly available in sizes and colors which seem to satisfy the requirements of most fly tiers. A beginner would do well to start by using a size 3/0 thread for larger flies, where strength is required. The smaller thread sizes, from 6/0 to 8/0 are best for the majority of smaller flies, including all dry flies. You must learn how to use these finer threads without breaking them, as they are indispensable to producing quality flies. Some threads are already lightly waxed when you purchase them; this is a convenience as such thread is less slippery.

BODY MATERIALS—Are those materials produced in a form that can be simply wrapped onto a hook shank to create the body of a fly. Tinsel is a flat metallic colored tape, usually gold or silver, and available in fine, medium, and wide sizes. Originally constructed of thin metal, a mylar plastic tinsel is now frequently used because it doesn't have sharp edges and doesn't tarnish. Oval tinsel in similar colors and sizes is also specified for bodies and ribbing. Wool of all sorts is used, especially on wet flies and streamers, since it tends to absorb water and sinks well. Orlon, acrylic, antron and polypropylene yarns are all used in fly tying. Floss is made of silk, nylon, or acetate and is used mostly for sinking flies. It's sold in a variety of colors. Spun fur is usually rabbit fur made into a yarn in various dyed colors. It's easy to work with and has a fuzzy appearance desirable on many flies. A special mohair blend is used for leech imitations. Chenille of nylon or rayon is sold in many sizes and colors and is best for sinking flies. Latex comes in sheet form which can be cut into strips and dyed or marked various colors. It sinks rapidly and is effective on many nymph patterns. New plastic materials, like larva lace or swannundaze or edge brite, provide fly tiers with an ever growing array of new fly tying possibilities.

FEATHERS—Are widely used in fly tying and probably every imaginable type of feather has been tried at one time or another. Hackle refers to feathers from the neck of a bird, most commonly a rooster. For dry flies a long, glossy, stiff hackle is desirable; for wet flies a soft, dull hackle is more appropriate. Hackles from grouse or partridge or other birds are often short and soft, and are referred to as "soft hackles." Extra long, thin hackles from the rump of a rooster are called "saddle hackles" and are used for streamer flies and larger drys. Quills generally refer to the primary or secondary wing quills of any bird. Goose, duck, and turkey quills, in either natural or dyed colors, are commonly used for tails and wings on a variety of flies. Tail feathers of some birds are used, mostly turkey, peacock and ringneck pheasant. The crest is the topmost feathers on the head of the bird. Golden pheasant crest feathers are frequently specified in fly patterns. Tippets refer to the barred feathers from the lower neck of the golden and amherst pheasants. Herl is part of a peacock or ostrich plume which has a long flexible stem and very short barbules. Peacock herl, with its metallic sheen, is an important fly tying ingredient. Marabou was originally a soft stork feather, but now refers to the long downy under-feather from turkeys. It's often used as a replacement for streamer wings due to its undulating motion in water. Flank feathers from the sides of wooduck, teal, pintail, and mallard ducks are one of the most popular fly wing materials. Body feathers of all descriptions are used from time to time and may be referred to as back feathers, breast feathers, or rump feathers. Best known to fly tiers are those from silver and ringneck pheasants, Hungarian partridge, as well as various ducks.

TAILS—An assortment of animal tails provides the fly tier with an inexpensive supply of materials that have the qualities of length and/or stiffness. Bucktails, usually from the whitetail deer species, provide a readily dyed source of hair used for the "bucktail" flies, for dry fly wings and other purposes. It's best to avoid the extremely crinkled hair. Calftails have a finer and more translucent hair used frequently for dry fly wings, and often substituted for bucktail. Again, avoid hair that is extremely crinkled and curled. Squirrel tails of either the gray or red species have a fine straight hair and are also used in dyed colors. Mink tails, in a range of natural and dyed colors, have been used for their stiff guard hairs which are excellent for dry fly tails and caddisfly wings. Woodchuck tails are used in the same manner as mink tails.

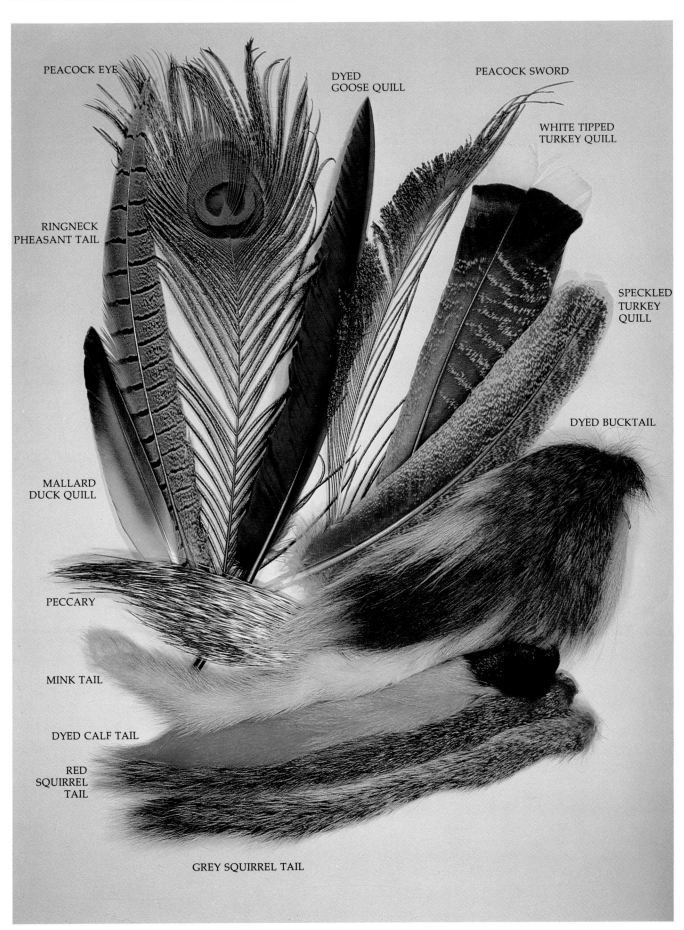

PEACOCK EYE

DYED
GOOSE QUILL

PEACOCK SWORD

WHITE TIPPED
TURKEY QUILL

RINGNECK
PHEASANT TAIL

SPECKLED
TURKEY
QUILL

MALLARD
DUCK QUILL

DYED BUCKTAIL

PECCARY

MINK TAIL

DYED CALF TAIL

RED
SQUIRREL
TAIL

GREY SQUIRREL TAIL

MATERIALS

HAIR—This category refers to the stiffer hairs, from the bodies of various animals. Most body hair of certain animals, specifically deer, antelope, caribou, elk and moose, is stiff and generally hollow. It's used in various ways for tails, wings, spun bodies and heads on many flies. It is important to use the proper hair for each purpose since each skin will have hair that's soft or stiff, short or long, and coarse or fine. Guard hairs (i.e. long stiffer hair as distinguished from short soft underfur) of various animals such as badger, black bear, grey fox and woodchuck are occasionally used for streamer or salmon fly wings. Some long, softer "streamer hairs" such as ram's wool have become popular too.

FURS—Mostly used as dubbing materials to form bodies, furs of all types and description are a basic material for fly tiers. Colors can be mixed and blended to provide any shade desired. Unprocessed furs, particularly from water-dwelling animals such as muskrat, otter, and beaver, contain natural oils which makes them resistant to water absorption. Furs when washed, bleached, or dyed lose this quality. Very fine furs such as rabbit and beaver are easiest to work with and available in many natural and dyed colors. A medium texture fur would be Australian possum, which combines general ease of use plus a rougher texture to often give a buggy effect. Seal fur is a very coarse and somewhat difficult fur to use properly; it, and its substitutes, have a sheen and translucency which makes for a brighter fly. Fur from a European hare's mask goes into the popular Hare's Ear dry fly, wet fly, and nymph.

SYNTHETICS—The non-availability or expense of many materials, combined with the growing variety of nylon, acrylic, rayon, dynel, kodel, mylar, polypropylene, and many other synthetics has led to substitution, experimentation, and frequently improvement. Leading the list of synthetics today must be the variety of synthetic furs on the market. These are being offered in various textures and colors selected especially for fly tiers. One must match the particular synthetic to its intended use to obtain the desired qualities. Polypropylene (poly) as a dubbing fur is lighter than water, but this advantage is offset by hook weight unless the fly has the additional support of a tail and hackle. Synthetics like this do not, however, become waterlogged and dry off when casting. Conversely, when synthetics are used on heavier wet fly hooks they tend to sink faster than natural furs. Imitation seal fur, imitation polar bear, and imitation bucktail have all proved their usefulness. Synthetic yarns, while already accepted in many forms, are finding increased usage as technology advances. Sparkle yarn comes to us via DuPont and offers the fly tier more light reflection. Poly yarn has been utilized for dry fly wings, and now Z-lon

and some sheet plastics are also finding a place in fly tying. Imitation jungle cock replaces the natural feather from the jungle fowl, a bird on the Endangered Species list. Nylon raffia is a straw-like material which can be used for dry fly wings or the wing cases on nymphs. The use of various closed-cell foams have revolutionized some of the floating flies by making them impossible to sink. For adding flash and glitter to a fly nothing beats the use of Crystal Flash or Flashabou. The list of new man-made materials could go on extensively, but many are still experimental, while others are being introduced each year.

OTHER MATERIALS—In order to add weight to flies, lead wire in various sizes is tied onto or wrapped around the hook shank; the addition of lead dumbbell eyes has resulted in some great deep-sinking fly patterns. Substitutes for the toxic lead have also been introduced. To help secure portions of the fly and make it more durable, a flexible adhesive cement such as vinyl cement is useful. It can also be applied to wing quill segments to prevent splitting. Head cement or lacquer, either clear or colored, is essential to coat the thread windings at the head of a fly upon completion to prevent loosening, and colored finishes are used for painted eyes. Modern fly tiers have found plenty of uses for the so-called "super glues," while epoxy and silicone have become important to the tiers of flies for salt water. Dubbing wax of a semi-tacky consistency is used when making fur dubbed bodies. Waterproof markers in a range of colors permit instant dying of some materials, or the addition of realistic markings on some flies.

There is no limit to the variety of materials and techniques used in creating flies for fishing. Fly tiers are constantly searching for new and better ways of producing imitations that catch fish. Perhaps this creative effort is part of the reason that fly tying has proved to be such an enjoyable hobby for so many people.

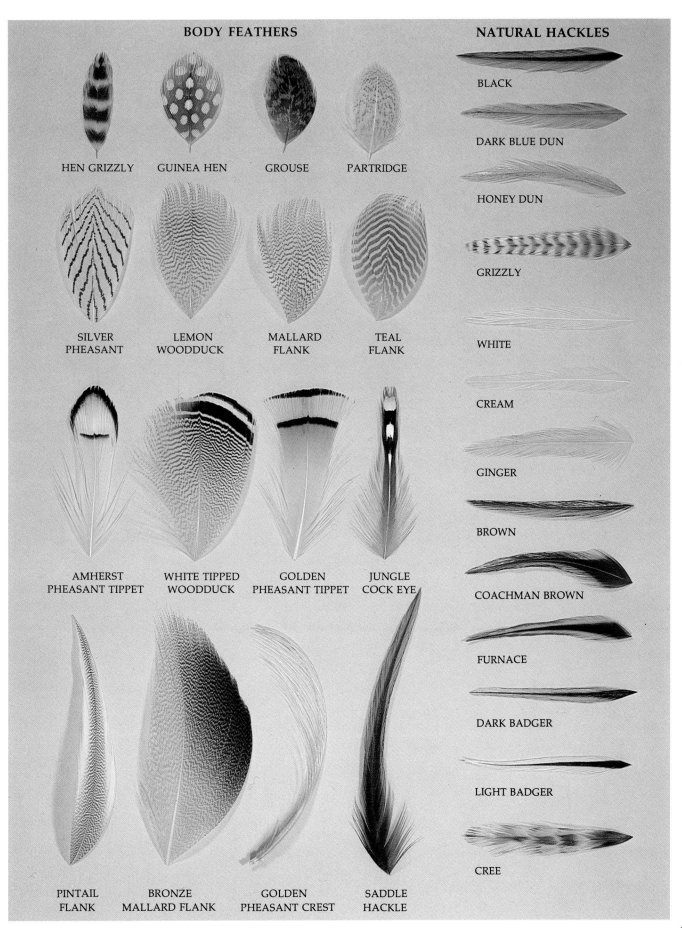

BODY FEATHERS

HEN GRIZZLY

GUINEA HEN

GROUSE

PARTRIDGE

SILVER
PHEASANT

LEMON
WOODDUCK

MALLARD
FLANK

TEAL
FLANK

AMHERST
PHEASANT TIPPET

WHITE TIPPED
WOODDUCK

GOLDEN
PHEASANT TIPPET

JUNGLE
COCK EYE

PINTAIL
FLANK

BRONZE
MALLARD FLANK

GOLDEN
PHEASANT CREST

SADDLE
HACKLE

NATURAL HACKLES

BLACK

DARK BLUE DUN

HONEY DUN

GRIZZLY

WHITE

CREAM

GINGER

BROWN

COACHMAN BROWN

FURNACE

DARK BADGER

LIGHT BADGER

CREE

PROPORTIONS

TRADITIONAL FLY PROPORTIONS

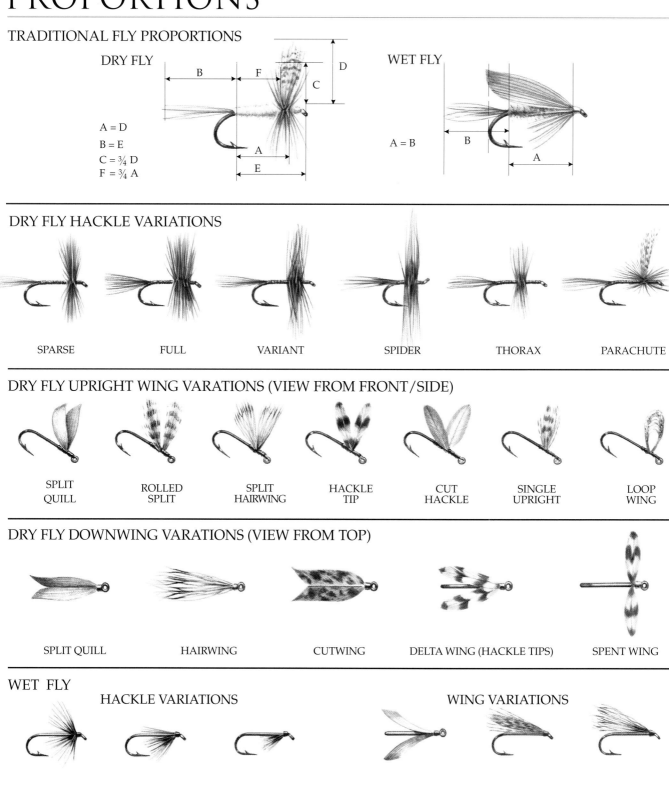

DRY FLY

B   F   D
C

A = D
B = E
C = ¾ D
F = ¾ A

A
E

WET FLY

A = B   B

A

DRY FLY HACKLE VARIATIONS

SPARSE   FULL   VARIANT   SPIDER   THORAX   PARACHUTE

DRY FLY UPRIGHT WING VARATIONS (VIEW FROM FRONT/SIDE)

SPLIT QUILL   ROLLED SPLIT   SPLIT HAIRWING   HACKLE TIP   CUT HACKLE   SINGLE UPRIGHT   LOOP WING

DRY FLY DOWNWING VARATIONS (VIEW FROM TOP)

SPLIT QUILL   HAIRWING   CUTWING   DELTA WING (HACKLE TIPS)   SPENT WING

WET FLY

HACKLE VARIATIONS

COLLAR   COLLAR (TIED DOWN)   BEARD

WING VARIATIONS

SPLAYED (TOP VIEW)   ROLLED   HAIRWING

SALMON AND STEELHEAD FLY VARIATIONS

STANDARD   REDUCED   LOW WATER

In the past there were few brands of hooks available to the fly tier and fly recipes often specified a single hook model for each fly. Today such a simple approach is complicated by the availability of many different brands of high quality hooks. Retail suppliers of fly tying materials limit their offerings because of the high cost of trying to stock all available models, so the fly tier must be able to substitute a hook which enables him to produce a fly which will perform as expected. Another factor to be considered by the fly tier is that there is no single best hook for all sizes of a particular fly pattern. For example, for a dry fly like the Adams I normally use a standard dry fly hook when tying the fly in sizes 14 to 18. On larger flies I prefer a light wire hook because it provides better flotation yet still offers adequate strength for trout. For sizes smaller than size 18 a straight eye hook avoids the potential hooking interference of a down-eye hook. Thus, for this single dry fly pattern I use three different hook styles.

HOOK EQUIVALENCE CHART

This chart is intended to serve as a basic guide to selecting those hooks most widely available to fly tiers through retail stores and mail order catalogs. It is by no means complete, and it does not include many of the specialty or single-purpose hooks. Because of subtle distinctions between many hooks, in color, barb, eye, shape, bend and sizing, it is not possible to make exact comparisons; yet this is exactly what this chart attempts to do. Also, the descriptions do not reflect the multiple uses of many hooks. For the most part, however, you should be able to rely on this information for basic hook selection.

	MANUFACTURER			
	Daiichi	Mustad	Partridge	Tiemco
Standard dry fly	1170, 1180	94840	L2A	5210
Std. dry fly, light wire	1100	94833	L3A, L4A	5230
Std. dry fly, heavy wire	-	7957B	A	9300
Std. dry fly, 2x long	1280	94831	H1A	5212
Std. dry fly, 1x short	1310	94836, 94838	E6A	921
Standard wet fly/nymph	1550	3906	G3A	9300
Standard wet fly, heavy wire	1530	3908	-	3769
Wet fly/nymph, 1x long	1560	3906B	-	3761
Wet fly/nymph, 2x long	1710	9671	SH2	5262
Wet fly/nymph, 3x long	1720	9672, 38941	SH3	5263
Bucktail/streamer, 4x long	2220	79580	D4A	9395
Bucktail/streamer, 6x long	2340, J171	3665A, 9575	CS17	300
Streamer, 8x long	-	94720	CS15	-
Salmon/steelhead, dry	-	9049	01, CS42	7989
Salmon/steelhead, wet	2421, 2161	90240	N, CS10	-
Salmon/steelhead, heavy	2441	36890	M	7999
Saltwater, short shank	2546	3407, 34007	-	800S, 811S
Saltwater, long shank	-	34011	CS11	-
SPECIALTY HOOKS				
Caddis/sedge	1130, 1140	37160	K12ST	205BL
Swimming nymph	1770	80150	K6ST	400T
Bass bug/wide gape	2720	37187, 3366	CS41	8089
Midge	1110	94859	K1A	101
Shrimp/grub	1150	80250	K2B, K4A	2457, 2487

Assorted hooks shown at actual size.

GLOSSARY

Aftershaft—soft, secondary feather, underlying the body feathers of pheasants and other birds

Attractor—usually a brightly colored fly which does not imitate any natural food, but is simply attractive to fish

Badger—a hackle with a black center stripe, see page 9; also refers to fur from animal of the same name

Barb—part of a hook, see page 5; also the individual fibers attached to the stem of a feather

Barbless—a hook without a barb

Barbule—miniature fibers along a feather barb

Barred—feather with parallel dark markings across width

Bend—see description of hooks, page 5

Beard—a style of applying throat hackle, see page 10

Biot—barb from the short side of a large wing quill

Bobbin—tool used to hold tying thread, see page 4

Bobbin Threader—tool to start thread through bobbin tube

Bodkin—a needle-like tool with handle, see page 4

Braided Tinsel—mylar braided around large cotton cord

Bucktail—hair from tail of deer; also a style of fly which uses bucktail as principal material

Butt—a part of fly, see page 13; also the ends of hair or feathers nearest the skin

CA Cement—any of the so-called "super glues"

CDC—see Cul de Canard

Caddisfly—type of common aquatic insect important to anglers, holds wings down over body

Caddis Hook—shaped hook to tie caddis larva and pupa imitations, sometimes called English Bait Hook

Cement—also called head cement or head lacquer, used to secure, preserve, and finish thread windings at head of fly

Collar—hackle or hair, wound as throat, see page 10

Covert—another term for wingcase on nymphs

Cree—a hackle of mixed white, brown, and gray markings

Crest—feather from top/back of pheasant neck

Cul de Canard—soft, oily feather from a duck's rump

Cut Wing—hackle or breast feather cut to shape of wing

Delta Wing—style of downwing fly, see page 10

Downwing—fly style with wings over the body

Dry Fly—artificial fly which floats upon water surface

Dubbing—a technique of applying fur; also refers to the fur itself, see page 25

Dubbing Teaser—tool used to pick out fur dubbing

Dubbing Twister—tool used to spin fur in a dubbing loop

Dun—see color plates; also first stage of adult mayfly

Egg Sack—imitates eggs found at rear of female insect

Emerger—an insect in the process of changing from nymph or pupa to adult

Embossed Tinsel—tinsel with reflective indentations

Epoxy—a two-part, very durable, cement

Eye—part of a hook, see page 5

Fanwing—style of dry fly wing using wide, fan-shaped breast feathers from a duck

Filoplume—usually refers to an aftershaft, which see

Flank—the side of a bird or duck

Floating Yarn—a polypropylene yarn

Flybody Hook—a hook style with a wire pointing rearward, used to make extended mayfly bodies

Furnace—a brown hackle with black center stripe

Gape—part of a hook measurement, see page 5

Gills—breathing parts of nymphs, usually on abdomen

Guard Hair—stiffer, longer hairs on skin of fur bearers

Hackle—feather from neck or back of bird, most frequently from rooster neck unless otherwise specified

Hackle Pliers—a tool used to grip hackle, see page 4

Hair Stacker—tool used to align hair tips, see page 5

Hairwing—a fly using any of various hairs for wing

Halfhitch—the simplest knot used to secure thread

Hen—a female chicken, pheasant or duck

Herl—short fibers on stem of peacock or ostrich plume

Horns—part of some classic salmon flies, tied on top of wings

Hot Colors—colors with high fluorescent intensity in sunlight

Jungle Cock—endangered wild fowl from Asia; imitations of its neck feathers (eyes) now in use

Keel Hook—a hook style designed to be weedless

Lacquer—a head cement, usually offered in colors

Larva—first immature stage of insects having a complete life cycle, e.g.. caddisfly. See also pupa and nymph

Latex—thin flat rubber sheets, usually tan or dyed

Limerick—a style of hook, see page 5

Loop Eye—style of hook eye, see page 5

Married—procedure whereby wing quill segments of same curvature are joined together edgewise

Material Bobbin—tool to dispense spooled materials

Mayfly—a family of insects common in freshwater, of significant importance to anglers

Midge—commonly refers to very small two-winged insects

Model Perfect—a style of hook, see page 5

Monocord—a flat, untwisted nylon thread

Monofilament—single strand, clear nylon fishing line

Mylar—flat metallic colored plastic ribbon or tape, used as a non tarnishing tinsel

Neck—the complete skin with hackle feathers from chicken, most frequently a rooster

Nymph—immature aquatic first stage of insects with incomplete life cycle. Longevity from 1 to 3 years

Oval Tinsel—a tinsel wrapped around a cotton thread

Packer—tool used to tightly pack bunches of deer body hair

Palmer—hackle wrapped over body of fly

Parachute—style of applying dry fly hackle, see page 10

Prewaxed—thread which has been waxed at the factory

Pupa—the second stage in the life cycle of insects having a complete life cycle; see also larva and nymph

Quill—commonly refers to feathers from the wing of a bird; also the stem of any feather

Reduced—a fly reduced in size from standard, often through the elimination of non-essential materials; see page 10

Rotary Vise—vise which revolves hook on center, thereby reducing amount of arm and hand motion required

Saddle—the rear back portion of a chicken

Schlappen—Long back hackles, similar to saddle hackles, but thick and very webby

Sculpin—a common, bottom-dwelling, bait fish

Shank—part of a hook, see page 5

Shellback—fly with material pulled over top of body thus forming a back

Shuck—the shed exoskeleton of an insect

Smelt—a small baitfish common in the Northeast

Soft Hackle—a short, soft, webby hackle for wet flies, usually hen, partridge, or grouse hackle

Sparse—indicates materials applied very sparingly

Spent Wing—a downwing style, see page 10

Spey—a river in Scotland after which a fly style was named

Spinner—last stage of adult mayfly life cycle

Spinning—the most common technique for applying deer body hair

Splayed—position of wings or tail when they are set to each side of the hook in a "V" shape

Split Bead—hollow metal bead, split open on one side

Sproat—a style of hook, see page 5

Spun Fur—fur, usually rabbit, made into yarn

Stem—the center supporting quill of a feather, actually a shaft

Stacker—see Hair Stacker

Stacking—process of evening the tips of hair

Stonefly—a family of large aquatic insects, the nymphal stage is of great importance to anglers

Streamer—type of fly designed to imitate small fish, usually made of feathers

Stripped—feather from which barbs have been removed

Synthetic—man-made, as opposed to natural, material such as Antron, Flashabou, Crystal Flash, Zing, Z-lon, Poly, FisHair, Acrylic, Ultra Hair, Larva Lace etc.

Tandem—two hooks, one trailing the other, connected by monofilament or wire

Tinsel—metal or metallic plastic ribbon-like material

Tippet—pheasant feather from lower neck and upper back

Underfur—soft fur nearest skin, shorter than guard hair

Upright—a style of wing, see page 10

Variant—a style of dry fly hackle, see page 10; also used to describe multicolored necks

Vinyl Cement—a very adhesive thin cement

Web—the soft, dull, webby lower center portion of hackle, undesirable for dry flys because it absorbs water

Weedguard—an attachment, often monofilament, incorporated into a fly to prevent the hook from catching weeds

Weighted—a fly with lead wire wrapped or tied on shank

Wet Fly—a traditional style of fly that sinks in water

Whip Finish—the best knot for finishing flies, see page 18

Wing Burner—a tool used to shape feathers

NOMENCLATURE

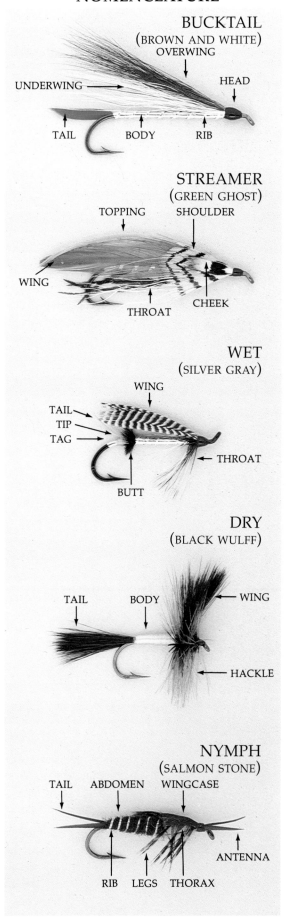

BUCKTAIL
(BROWN AND WHITE)
OVERWING
UNDERWING
HEAD
TAIL   BODY   RIB

STREAMER
(GREEN GHOST)
TOPPING   SHOULDER
WING
THROAT   CHEEK

WET
(SILVER GRAY)
WING
TAIL
TIP
TAG
THROAT
BUTT

DRY
(BLACK WULFF)
TAIL   BODY   WING
HACKLE

NYMPH
(SALMON STONE)
TAIL   ABDOMEN   WINGCASE
ANTENNA
RIB   LEGS   THORAX

BUCKTAILS

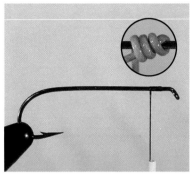

1. Place bend of hook securely in vise. Starting 1/8th inch from eye of hook, hold thread in left hand, bobbin in right hand, and place thread against hook. Using your right hand, wrap the thread over itself several times as shown. Cut away loose end.

6. With the left hand, take a firm hold of the positioned bucktail and wrap the thread 6 to 8 times tightly around the bunch, keeping it on top of the hook shank and making sure not to wrap too close to the hook eye.

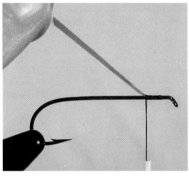

2. Cut a 4 to 6 inch piece of tinsel to a tapered end. Place the end directly over the thread wraps, then secure the tinsel by wrapping it down with 4 or 5 turns of thread.

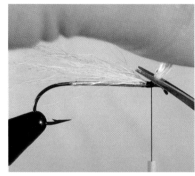

7. Using scissors, trim the excess bucktail ends on an angle as shown.

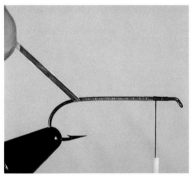

3. Wind the tinsel in close turns to the rear of the hook, leaving no space between turns, but not overlapping.

8. Repeat steps 5, 6, and 7, using red bucktail, and repeat again using a few strands of peacock herl on top.

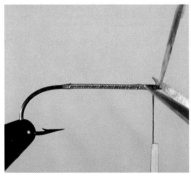

4. Wrap the tinsel forward in the same manner, thus forming a smooth even body. Once the tinsel is returned forward, wrap it down with 4 or 5 turns of thread and trim away excess tinsel.

9. Wrap down all the ends to form a neat, tapered head. Make 3 or 4 tight half-hitch knots as shown and cut away the thread close to the head.

5. Cut a small bunch of white bucktail; align the tips to eliminate stray hairs. Holding the bunch in your right hand, position it near the eye of the hook to measure the desired length. It should extend just a bit beyond the bend of the hook.

10. Using a bodkin or needle, apply head lacquer or cement and let dry. Repeat several times until a smooth, glossy finish is achieved.

STREAMERS

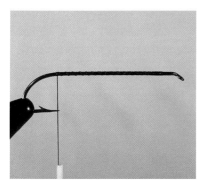

1. Provide a thread base by beginning behind the hook eye and wrapping your thread tightly to the end of the hook shank.

2. Select a bunch of yellow barbs for tail material and position them so the tail length equals the size of the hook gape. Secure the tail with 3 or 4 wraps of thread and cut away excess.

3. Cut lengths of wool and tinsel, each about 4 to 5 inches; lay both over the length of the hook shank to about 1/4 inch behind the eye and wrap thread several times at rear, then wrap thread forward making a smooth foundation.

4. Wrap wool tightly forward, tie it down, and cut off excess.

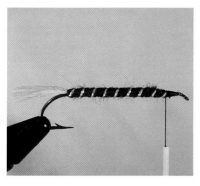

5. Spiral the tinsel forward in open turns to form the rib, tie down and clip away any excess.

6. Strip a bunch of barbs from a large hackle dyed yellow. Hold these under the the hook with your left hand as you bind them in place with thread, and trim away the butt ends.

7. For the wing select a pair of white saddle or streamer hackles. Place them together with concave sides facing each other, determine desired length, and strip away excess barbs.

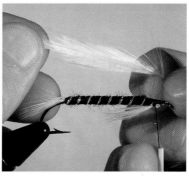

8. Holding the wing hackles together in the left hand, crimp the base of the feathers by placing the stems on the right index finger and pressing firmly with the right thumbnail.

9. Place wing on top of hook, secure at the crimped spot with several wraps of thread, and trim away excess stems.

10. Position one jungle cock eye on each side of the wing, wrap in place, and trim ends. Tie off thread using half hitches or a whip finish and apply head cement.

BUGGERS

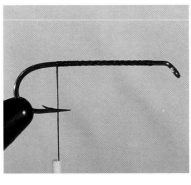

1. Wind a base of thread the length of the hook shank, leaving a space of at least 1/8th inch behind the hook eye. Move the thread to the rear.

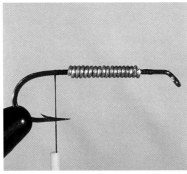

2. Tightly wrap lead wire over the center 2/3rds of the hook shank.

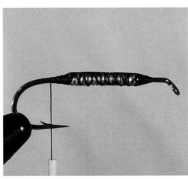

3. Using your thread, secure the lead in place and build up a smooth taper at the front and back of the lead. Coat the lead with cement or lacquer to prevent discoloration later.

4. Strip a bunch of fibers from a marabou feather and tie in as a tail. Do not include the feather stem unless it is extremely soft and pliable.

5. Attach 4 to 5 inch lengths of wire and chenille at the rear of the hook.

6. Select a saddle hackle or long, soft neck hackle and attach it by its tip, with the shiny side facing forward. Move the thread to the front.

7. Wrap the chenille forward and tie down in front. The first wrap of chenille should be made behind the attachment point of the hackle.

8. Wrap the hackle forward in widely spaced turns, taking one extra wrap when you reach the head of the fly. As you wrap, maintain the shiny side forward; this will make the individual barbs slant toward the rear.

9. Wrap the wire forward in a direction opposite the direction used to wind the hackle. These wraps bind the delicate hackle stem. Secure the wire with thread and break the wire by wiggling it back and forth.

10. Cut away any excess materials, wrap a smooth head and cement.

NYMPHS

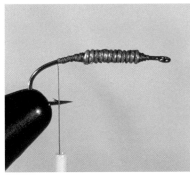

1. Start your thread and wrap the length of the hook shank. Cut a 3" to 4" length of lead wire, wrap it around the center 2/3 of the hook shank and secure with numerous wraps of thread.

2. Select a few barbs of a lemon woodduck flank feather and tie in at the rear of the hook. Attach a 4" piece of fine oval gold tinsel.

3. From a hare's mask cut some light and dark mottled fur from around the base of the ears and mix together for your dubbing blend.

4. Apply a small amount of dubbing to your waxed thread and wrap an abdomen over the rear 60 percent of the hook shank. See page 25 for a description of dubbing techniques.

5. Reverse wrap the tinsel over the abdomen in wide, open turns. Secure the tinsel and trim away any excess.

6. Attach the material selected for a wingpad. Usually this is a wing quill segment of speckled turkey or natural goose, or else a flashback material such as crystal flash or Flashabou.

7. Apply a slightly heavier amount of dubbing to form the thorax.

8. Pull the wingpad material tightly over the top of the thorax. Tie down at the head.

9. Cut away all excess material, wrap a head, tie off, and apply head cement.

10. Using a dubbing needle, or a dubbing teaser, pick out some of the fur from the thorax. This will represent the legs of a nymph.

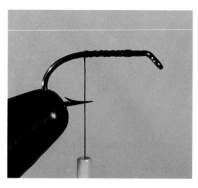

1. Begin by wrapping a thread foundation.

6. Pull the hackle down and back as shown, and secure it in this position with 3 or 4 turns of thread.

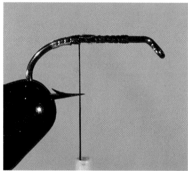

2. At the tail position attach a 3" to 4" length of tinsel. Wrap 2 or 3 turns toward the rear, then reverse direction and wind forward to the original tie-in point. Secure and cut away excess tinsel.

7. Select 2 wing quill segments, one each from a matched pair of natural gray duck wing quills.

3. Attach 2 to 4 strands of peacock herl at the rear, then wind them forward in close turns to form a body. Trim away any excess. Some tiers like to reinforce the herl body with fine gold wire, or thread, or cement.

8. Holding both wing segments tightly on top of the hook shank, bring the thread up between your thumb and the wing, over the wing, and down the other side and under the hook; then apply tension as you begin a second similar wrap.

4. Attach a soft, webby, brown hackle as shown, and clip away excess.

9. Trim away any excess material and wrap a head. Lay a loop of separate thread as shown and wrap over it 4 or 5 times with the tying thread.

5. Wrap the hackle 2 or 3 turns, tie down, and cut away excess.

10. Cut the tying thread leaving a 2" to 3" end which is inserted through the loop. Pull on the cut ends of the loop thus bringing tying thread under itself. This produces a whip finish knot.

DRY FLIES

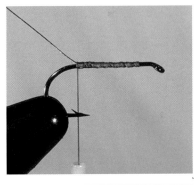

1. Begin by forming a thread base, and attach a length of fine gold wire at the rear.

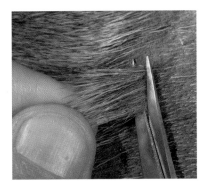

6. Cut a bunch of straight elk hair from the skin and align the tips using a hair stacker.

2. Dub a fur body as shown. Colors usually match a natural caddisfly, frequently in shades of olive, brown, gray or tan.

7. Holding the elk hair in your right hand, measure it against the length of the hook.

3. At the front of the body attach a dry fly hackle as shown, concave side to the rear, shiny side forward.

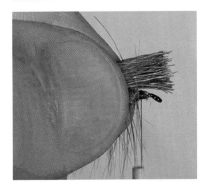

8. Once the length of the elk hair has been determined, switch hands and hold it in position with your left hand.

4. Wind the hackle to the rear with 4 to 6 winds.

9. Gripping it firmly on top, tie down the elk hair with several tight turns of thread.

5. Holding the hackle tips with the left hand make 2 tight turns of wire at the rear, then spiral the wire forward to secure the hackle. Tie off the wire and break off excess. Cut away the excess hackle tips.

10. Tie off and trim the butt ends of the elk hair as shown. Cement.

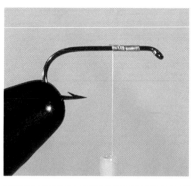

1. Wrap a thread base at the wing position as shown.

6. Dub a very small ball of fur at the rear of the hook shank. The color is chosen to match the lighter underside of a mayfly.

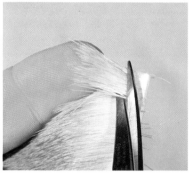

2. Select some fine, straight deer body hair for the wing. Usually coastal deer hair or stacked yearling elk is best. Keep the tips even as you cut from the hide.

7. Tie in a tail of Microfibetts or stiff hackle on the far side of the body. (Optionally, some tiers are using a single short tail of a bunch of Z-Lon. This is intended to represent the nymphal shuck of an emerging mayfly.)

3. Tightly tie the deer body hair on top of the hook shank, tips pointed forward.

8. Tie in a near side tail in the same manner.

4. Push the wing upright and make several turns of thread in front of the base of the wing to keep it upright. Viewed from the front, the wing should splay a full 180 degrees.

9. Prepare a long, thin length of fur dubbing.

5. Trim the butt ends to a gradual taper, wrap and move thread to the rear.

10. Wrap the dubbing the full length of the body to the hook eye and tie off.

DRY FLIES

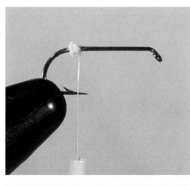

1. Dub a very small ball of fur at the rear of the hook shank.

6. Tie in the hackle at the wing position.

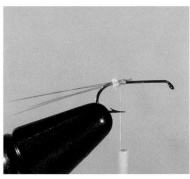

2. Attach a fairly long tail on each side using either Microfibetts or other thin, stiff fibers.

7. Wrap the hackle at the wing position, leaving space at the front of the hook. Tie off and trim away excess.

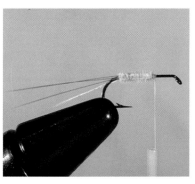

3. Prepare a length of very thin fur dubbing, color to match the color of a natural mayfly spinner.

8. Apply more dubbing in front of the wing to complete the body.

4. Wind the dubbing forward to cover the rear 60 percent of the hook shank.

9. Tie off.

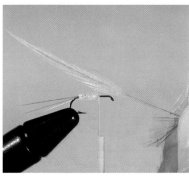

5. Select a light blue dun dry fly hackle, or stiff saddle hackle, and strip away the lower webby portion. This hackle may be somewhat oversize. On large flies you may need to use two hackles.

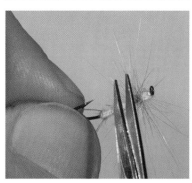

10. Remove the hook from your vise and trim the hackle flat on the bottom so it will float flush on the water surface. Cutting it flat on top is optional.

21

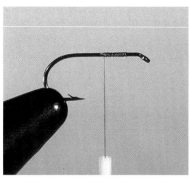

1. Begin by forming a thread base at the point of wing attachment. Use a fine olive thread.

2. Tie in a section of woodduck flank, or mallard dyed wood-duck, tips pointing forward, and trim away the excess butt ends to a smooth taper.

3. Pull the wing upright and make several thread turns immediately in front to hold the wing up.

4. Divide the wing into 2 equal bunches and criss-cross the thread through the middle. This results in an upright divided wing.

5. Depending on the size and fullness of the fly, and the length of your hackles, select one or two blue dun dry fly hackles; strip away the soft lower barbs, and attach behind the wing as shown.

6. Move the thread to rear and attach a few stiff blue dun hackle barbs, forming a tail as shown.

7. Select a long hackle from a red-brown neck. Strip away all of the barbs and soak the stem in warm water until pliable. Tie in the fine end at the tail position and move your thread to just behind the wing.

8. Wind the stripped hackle stem forward in ajoining turns, to a point just behind the wings. It will form a body with a natural taper. Tie down, trim excess and move the thread forward.

9. Pull hackles upright, then wrap first hackle one or two turns behind wing and remaining turns in front of the wing. Tie down tip. Wrap the second hackle, mostly in front of wing, and tie down the tip.

10. Closely cut away tips, form a small head with very few turns of thread, and whip finish.

MUDDLERS

1. Cut a segment from a speckled turkey wing quill. For this fly we use a slightly heavier thread because of the tension needed when working with deer body hair.

6. Cut matched segments from a pair of speckled turkey wing quills and apply the wing on top, concave sides together, in the same manner as you would place a wet fly wing.

2. Tie in the turkey quill segment as a tail, curving downward. Wrapping the excess material along the hook shank avoids building a lump at the rear. Be sure to keep your materials on top of the hook shank.

7. Form a collar by tying on each side of the wing a collar from a bunch of natural gray/brown deer body hair, with the tips extending toward the rear. Advance your thread.

3. Move the thread forward about 2/3rds the shank length and attach a piece of flat gold tinsel.

8. For the head, spin 1 or 2 (depending on hook size) bunches of deer body hair, tightly packed. Tie off.

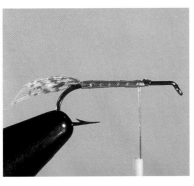

4. Wind the tinsel to the rear then reverse direction and wind back to the tie-in point. Tie down and cut away excess tinsel.

9. Using scissors or (carefully) a razor blade, shape the Muddler head as shown, being cautious not to cut into the collar.

5. Select a bunch of gray squirrel tail hair and tie in on top, forming an underwing. Some tiers substitute brown calftail or red squirrel. Squirrel tail hair is slippery, so apply a drop of cement. Trim away the butt ends.

10. The shape of the finished fly. The size and shape of the head varies according to individual preferences.

23

SCULPINS

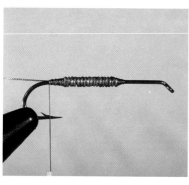

1. Make a thread base, wrap and secure lead wire if weight is desired, and attach a length of oval gold tinsel at the rear.

2. Dub a cream or tan body over the rear 1/2 of the hook shank. The color should match the color of the sculpins where this fly will be fished. For a light sandy riverbed, choose light colors.

3. From a hen back skin select 2 matched body feathers. Measure against the fly to determine proper length, and strip away excess barbs at base. Some tiers also strip away some of the barbs on the underside.

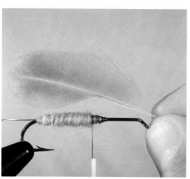

4. Tie in the pair of hen body feathers as ahown.

5. Pull the feather barbs upright so they can be easily separated with a dubbing needle, then wrap the oval tinsel. First make a full turn at the rear to secure the feathers, then make wide turns forward to the front of the body.

6. Trim away excess materials and dub a turn of red fur to represent gills.

7. Surround the upper body with a collar of sparse brown ram's wool, combed out, leaving some tips pointing to the rear.

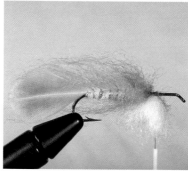

8. At the head, tie a bunch of white wool on the underside.

9. At the head, tie a bunch of brown wool on top. Repeat steps 8 & 9 as often as needed to fill in the remaining head area. Tie off.

10. Trim the head to a broad, flattened shape as shown.

Dubbing is probably the most useful technique in fly tying. It involves making a "yarn" out of natural or synthetic furs by applying and twisting them around waxed thread. Flies constructed with dubbed bodies have many advantages, such as better floating or sinking qualities (depending on the materials selected), greater realism, sparkle, movement, and the ability to mix and blend different colored furs to obtain specific colors. Most difficulties that fly tiers encounter are the result of applying too much fur, so begin by using very little.

SIMPLE TWISTED METHOD

1. After winding thread on hook, and applying tail if necessary, wax a 3 to 4 inch section of thread.

2. Very sparingly press small amounts of soft loose fur against the waxed thread, thin near the hook and slightly heavier below to form a taper.

3. Taking hold of fur between thumb and index finger, twist fur in one direction only, forming a tight noodle.

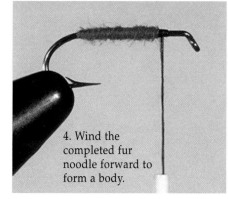

4. Wind the completed fur noodle forward to form a body.

SMOOTH LOOP METHOD

1. Form a 3 to 4 inch loop from a separate thread, secure to hook, and wax thread loop.

2. Insert small amounts of loose fur or synthetic between the two thread strands.

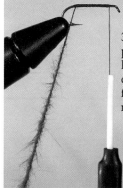

3. Attach hackle pliers to bottom of loop then spin in one direction, forming a tight noodle.

4. Wind the completed fur noodle forward to form a body.

ROUGH LOOP METHOD

1. To add a collar or thorax of rough dubbing, form a loop, wax, and insert fur clipped from skin, with guard hairs included, as shown. Clip the butt ends short.

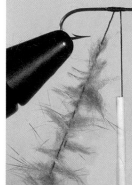

2. Attach hackle pliers to bottom of the loop and spin in one direction, thus securing fur.

3. Moisten your fingers and press the fur so it points rearward as shown.

. Wind the fur dubbing around the hook to form thorax or collar as desired.

COLOR GUIDE

This color guide is designed to show those colors most referred to by fly tiers and fly tying books. The particular shades used here were selected from hundreds of color hues on a consensus basis by a team of several long experienced tiers, and thus present an average interpretation. It might be noted that only rarely was there total agreement on a color.

Natural furs and feathers have properties such as translucency and blended tones we cannot reproduce in flat color chips, so some judgement should be exercised when making a direct comparison. The relative value of these colors should prove very useful in selecting materials, particularly to beginning tiers.

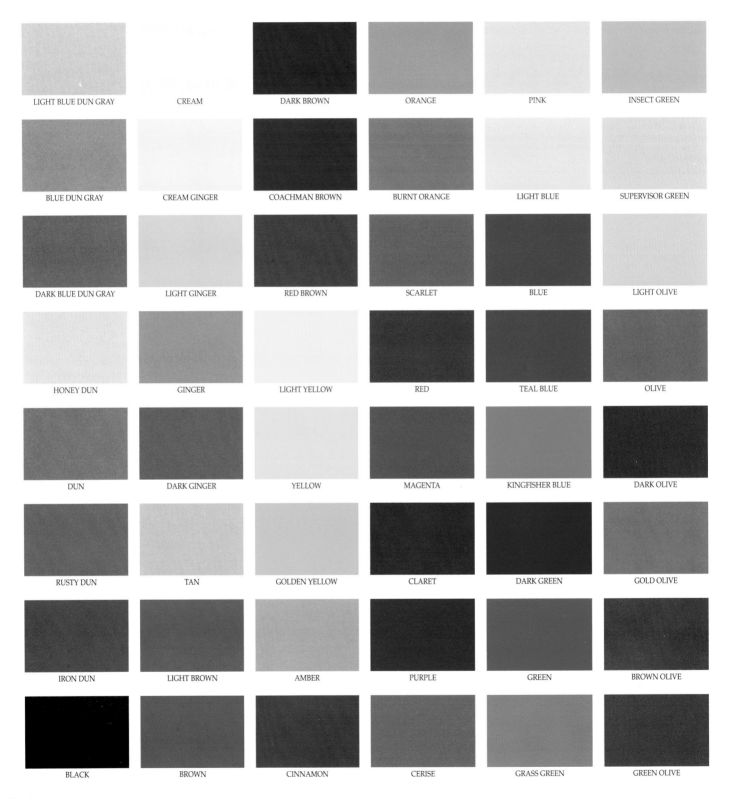

LIGHT BLUE DUN GRAY	CREAM	DARK BROWN	ORANGE	PINK	INSECT GREEN
BLUE DUN GRAY	CREAM GINGER	COACHMAN BROWN	BURNT ORANGE	LIGHT BLUE	SUPERVISOR GREEN
DARK BLUE DUN GRAY	LIGHT GINGER	RED BROWN	SCARLET	BLUE	LIGHT OLIVE
HONEY DUN	GINGER	LIGHT YELLOW	RED	TEAL BLUE	OLIVE
DUN	DARK GINGER	YELLOW	MAGENTA	KINGFISHER BLUE	DARK OLIVE
RUSTY DUN	TAN	GOLDEN YELLOW	CLARET	DARK GREEN	GOLD OLIVE
IRON DUN	LIGHT BROWN	AMBER	PURPLE	GREEN	BROWN OLIVE
BLACK	BROWN	CINNAMON	CERISE	GRASS GREEN	GREEN OLIVE

HOOK — *Standard dry fly; sizes 10 to 20*
THREAD — *Black*
TAIL — *Mixed grizzly and brown hackle barbs*
BODY — *Gray muskrat underfur*
WING — *Grizzly hackle tips*
HACKLE — *Mixed grizzly and brown*
COMMENT — *The Adams is probably the most popular dry fly in use today. In a variety of sizes, it belongs in everyone's fly box.*

ADAMS

HOOK — *Standard dry fly; sizes 10 to 16*
THREAD — *Brown*
TAIL — *Brown hackle barbs*
BODY — *Hackle is tied in at the rear of hook and closely wound forward. Often more than one hackle is required. At the front place 2 or 3 turns of white hackle to make the fly more visible*
COMMENT — *A high floating fly, the bivisible is particularly good in fast water. Other popular colors are blue dun, ginger, black and badger, all with white up front.*

BIVISIBLE (BROWN)

HOOK — *Standard dry fly; sizes 10 to 18*
THREAD — *Black*
TAIL — *Black hackle barbs*
BODY — *Black dubbed fur*
WING — *Slate gray mallard wing quill sections*
HACKLE — *Black*
COMMENT — *A popular dark fly which has many variations. It is very good as a midge pattern when tied without wings in small sizes, 20 to 24.*

BLACK GNAT

HOOK — *Standard dry fly; sizes 14 to 22*
THREAD — *Olive*
TAIL — *Blue dun Microfibetts or hackle barbs*
BODY — *Olive dubbed fur*
WING — *Dark blue dun Z-lon, loop wing style*
HACKLE — *Blue dun*
COMMENT — *Several mayfly species in the olive group have similar coloration, but sizes will vary greatly. Some anglers prefer a body color of a blend of 1/3 olive and 2/3 brown rabbit.*

BLUE WING OLIVE (LOOP WING)

HOOK — *Standard dry fly; sizes 12 to 16*
THREAD — *Tan*
TAIL — *Light blue dun Microfibetts*
BODY — *Light tannish olive-gray dubbing*
WING — *Gray-brown speckled partridge body feathers, tied upright, 1/3 way back from the hook eye*
HACKLE — *Grizzly, wound both behind and in front of the wing, clipped flat on the bottom*
HEAD — *Light tannish olive-gray dubbing*
COMMENT — *The thorax style moves the wing and hackle slightly toward the rear of the hook.*

CALLIBAETIS (THORAX)

CLASSIC DRY FLIES

CREAM VARIANT

HOOK — *Standard dry fly; sizes 12 to 20*
THREAD — *Yellow*
TAIL — *Cream hackle barbs*
BODY — *Stem from a cream hackle, well soaked, the small end tied in at the rear and wrapped forward*
WING — *None*
HACKLE — *Cream*
COMMENT — *All variants are tied with a hackle which is one size larger than the size normally selected for the hook size. See page 10.*

GRAY FOX

HOOK — *Standard dry fly; sizes 12 to 18*
THREAD — *Pale yellow*
TAIL — *Ginger hackle barbs*
BODY — *Tan colored fur from red fox*
WING — *Mallard flank*
HACKLE — *Mixed light ginger and light grizzly*

GREEN DRAKE (EXTENDED BODY)

HOOK — *Standard, or 1X long dry fly; sizes 8 to 12*
THREAD — *Olive*
TAIL — *Three moose mane hairs*
BODY — *Olive deer body hair, extended as shown*
RIB — *Olive tying thread*
WING — *Dark brown elk or similar stiff hair*
HACKLE — *Grizzly dyed olive, parachute style*
COMMENT — *Can also be tied with brown colors to represent the brown drake.*

GRIFFITH GNAT

HOOK — *Standard dry fly; sizes 14 to 22*
THREAD — *Black*
TAIL — *None*
BODY — *Peacock herl*
WING — *None*
HACKLE — *Grizzly, wrapped over the herl body*
RIB — *Fine gold wire (optional)*
COMMENT — *This fly pattern has proved to be a very effective imitation of small, dark midges.*

LIGHT CAHILL (PARACHUTE)

HOOK — *Standard dry fly; sizes 12 and 14*
THREAD — *Yellow*
TAIL — *Light ginger hackle barbs*
BODY — *Cream belly fur from red fox*
WING — *White calftail, a single upright clump*
HACKLE — *Light ginger to cream ginger. The hackle is wound around the base of the upright wing.*
COMMENT — *Almost any standard dry fly can be tied in the parachute style which helps the fly alight more softly upon the water.*

HOOK — *Standard dry fly; sizes 10 and 12*
THREAD — *Orange*
TAIL — *Ginger hackle barbs*
BODY — *Tan colored fur from a red fox*
WING — *Woodduck flank*
HACKLE — *Mixed dark ginger and dark grizzly*

MARCH BROWN

HOOK — *Standard dry fly; sizes 12 to 18*
THREAD — *Black*
TAIL — *Grizzly hackle barbs*
BODY — *Moose mane, one light strand and one dark strand wrapped together*
WING — *Grizzly hackle tips*
HACKLE — *Grizzly*
COMMENT — *For durability, coat the body with cement.*

MOSQUITO

HOOK — *Standard dry fly; sizes 12 to 18*
THREAD — *Olive*
TAIL — *Medium blue dun hackle barbs*
BODY — *Quill section from lower part of a peacock eye, stripped of herl and wrapped on to make a segmented body*
WING — *Woodduck flank*
HACKLE — *Medium blue dun*
COMMENT — *In the East the Quill Gordon is often the first mayfly to appear at streamside in the early spring.*

QUILL GORDON

HOOK — *Standard dry fly; sizes 10 to 18*
THREAD — *Olive*
TAIL — *Medium blue dun hackle barbs*
BODY — *Well soaked quill (stem) from reddish-brown hackle which has been stripped of barbs*
WING — *Woodduck flank*
HACKLE — *Medium blue dun*
COMMENT — *An excellent fly which resembles several mayfly species. It can be converted to a spinner by clipping the hackle top and bottom.*

RED QUILL

HOOK — *Short shank "spider hook" such as Mustad 94838 or 9523; sizes 12 to 18*
THREAD — *Black*
TAIL — *Badger hackle barbs*
HACKLE — *Oversize stiff badger hackle*
COMMENT — *Spiders are popular low-water flies; also tied in blue dun, black, brown and light ginger.*

**SPIDER
(BADGER)**

CLASSIC DRY FLIES

AUSABLE WULFF

HOOK — *Standard length to 2X long dry fly; sizes 8 to 16*
THREAD — *Fluorescent red*
TAIL — *Woodchuck tail*
BODY — *Cinnamon-rusty orange Australian possum fur dubbing*
WING — *White calftail*
HACKLE — *Mixed brown and grizzly*

GRAY WULFF

HOOK — *Standard length to 2X long dry fly; sizes 8 to 16*
THREAD — *Black*
TAIL — *Brown bucktail or elk*
BODY — *Bluish-gray spun fur or muskrat dubbing*
WING — *Brown bucktail or elk*
HACKLE — *Medium to dark blue dun*

GRIZZLY WULFF

HOOK — *Standard length to 2X long dry fly; sizes 8 to 16*
THREAD — *Black*
TAIL — *Brown bucktail or elk*
BODY — *Yellow floss or dubbed fur*
WING — *Brown bucktail*
HACKLE — *Mixed grizzly and brown*
COMMENT — *If floss is used for body, it should be lacquered after being wound in place.*

ROYAL WULFF

HOOK — *Standard length to 2X long dry fly; sizes 8 to 16*
THREAD — *Black*
TAIL — *Brown bucktail or elk*
BODY — *Rear 1/4 peacock herl, mid 1/2 red floss, front 1/4 peacock herl*
WING — *White calftail or bucktail*
HACKLE — *Coachman brown*

WHITE WULFF

HOOK — *Standard length to 2X long dry fly; sizes 8 to 16*
THREAD — *Black*
TAIL — *White bucktail or other stiff hair*
BODY — *Cream or off-white spun fur or dubbing*
WING — *White bucktail or other stiff hair*
HACKLE — *Light badger*

HOOK — *Standard length to 2X long dry fly; sizes 8 to 16*
THREAD — *Yellow*
TAIL — *Light elk*
BODY & WING — *Over rear 60% of shank tie in a clump of light elk hair, tips pointing rearward, twice the length of the body. Wrap thread tightly forward forming the body, then fold the elk hair over the body making a shellback, tie down in front of body. The tips are used to form upright divided wings*
HACKLE — *Mixed grizzly and brown*
COMMENT — *Also known as the Goofus Bug, this fly is tied with red, orange, green and fluorescent green bodies with dark elk used with dark bodies.*

HUMPY (YELLOW)

HOOK — *Standard length to 2X long dry fly; sizes 8 to 14*
THREAD — *Black*
TAIL — *Brown bucktail or elk*
BODY — *Spun gray-brown deer body hair clipped to shape as shown*
WING — *Brown bucktail or elk*
HACKLE — *Medium to dark blue dun, tied heavy*
COMMENT — *This is a good floating fly, but most beginning fly tiers find the construction difficult. It is also tied with the colors of an Adams.*

IRRESISTIBLE

HOOK — *Standard length to 2X long dry fly; sizes 8 to 16*
THREAD — *Black*
TAIL — *Golden pheasant tippets*
BODY — *Lime colored dubbing*
WING — *White calftail extending to middle of tail*
HACKLE — *Mixed brown and grizzly*
COMMENT — *One of many Trude patterns which are of similar construction; they are tied in various colors, often adaptations of standard dry flies like the Royal Coachman, Adams or Black Gnat.*

LIME TRUDE

HOOK — *Standard length to 2X long dry fly; sizes 8 to 16*
THREAD — *To match body color*
TAIL — *Natural light deer body hair*
BODY — *Fluorescent orange or yellow floss tied over the butt ends of the tail*
HEAD & WING — *Natural light deer body hair, tied reversed or bullethead style, with most of the deer hair pulled over the top to form a wing*
LEGS — *Round white rubber hackle, tied to form an X*
COMMENT — *This fly and its variations are rapidly becoming favorites in many areas; probably it's the motion of the rubber legs that makes it so effective.*

MADAME X

HOOK — *Curved nymph hook, 3X long; sizes 4 to 16*
THREAD — *Fluorescent orange*
TAIL — *Medium elk*
BODY — *Bright or rusty orange Haretron or Antron dubbing, palmered with a brown hackle*
RIB — *Gold wire*
WING — *Medium elk*
THORAX — *Amber dubbing*
HACKLE — *Grizzly, 3 or 4 turns through the thorax*
COMMENT — *Randall Kaufmann's design is tied in other colors to represent most downwing flies.*

STIMULATOR (ORANGE)

NO-HACKLE DRY FLIES

COMPARA-DUN

HOOK — *Standard length dry fly; sizes 8 to 22*
THREAD — *To match body color*
TAIL — *Micro Fibetts, split outrigger style*
BODY — *A blend of rabbit fur dubbing, the color of which is chosen so that when it becomes wet it will be the proper color to match the natural mayfly*
WING — *Light or dark (to match mayfly) natural coastal deer body hair, or straight, short hair from a deer mask or shoulder*
COMMENT — *The Compara-dun style has become one of the most widely accepted styles for imitating a variety of mayfly duns. It can be tied in any suitable color to match local hatches.*

COMPARA-SPINNER

HOOK — *Standard length dry fly; sizes 8 to 22*
THREAD — *To match body color*
TAIL — *Micro Fibetts, split outrigger style*
BODY — *A blend of rabbit fur dubbing, the color of which is chosen so that when it becomes wet it will be the proper color to match the natural mayfly. The body of a spinner imitation should be kept as thin as possible*
WING — *Light or dark hackle wound over the thorax portion of the body. The hackle is then trimmed very short, top and bottom*
COMMENT — *The Compara-spinner, like its dun counterpart, is a style which can be tied in any suitable color.*

HEN SPINNER

HOOK — *Standard length dry fly; sizes 8 to 22*
THREAD — *To match body color*
TAIL — *Hackle barbs or Micro Fibetts*
BODY — *Fur dubbing to match the natural mayfly*
WING — *The rounded tips of two hen hackle feathers, tied spent wing style, one to each side*
COMMENT — *Hen spinners are very realistic and are tied in many sizes and colors.*

NO-HACKLE

HOOK — *Standard length dry fly; sizes 14 to 22*
THREAD — *To match body color*
TAIL — *Hackle barbs or Micro Fibetts*
BODY — *Poly dubbing to match the natural mayfly*
WING — *Sections from a right and left wing feather of a mallard duck, attached sidewinder style*
COMMENT — *It takes a bit of practice to learn how to secure the wings perfectly, but once you master this you will have some of the best mayfly imitations.*

SPARKLE SPINNER

HOOK — *Standard length dry fly; sizes 12 to 22*
THREAD — *To match body color*
TAIL — *Hackle barbs or Micro Fibetts*
BODY — *Fur dubbing to match the natural mayfly, very thin*
WING — *One of the modern synthetics such as Z-lon or Crystal Flash or similar, clear or very light gray, tied spent wing style*
COMMENT — *The larger sizes require a stiffer wing material than the smaller flies.*

HOOK — *Standard length dry fly; sizes 10 to 18*
THREAD — *Brown*
BODY — *Ginger-olive dubbing*
HACKLE — *Ginger*
RIB — *Fine gold wire*
WING — *Elk hair (some tiers prefer deer hair)*
HEAD — *Butt ends of the wing, clipped short*
COMMENT — *For quiet water fishing a no-hackle version of this fly is quite simple to tie. Use colors to match local insects.*

ELK HAIR CADDIS

HOOK — *Standard length dry fly; sizes 10 to 16*
THREAD — *Gray or black*
BODY — *Natural deer body hair, spun and trimmed into the shape of a winged adult caddisfly*
ANTENNAE — *Two stems from a brown hackle, with the barbs removed*
HACKLE — *Brown*
COMMENT — *If desired, as a first step, a small loop of fur may be attached at the back, and later be pulled forward, underneath the body.*

GODDARD CADDIS

HOOK — *Standard length dry fly; sizes 12 to 18*
THREAD — *Olive*
BODY — *Light olive dubbing or floss*
RIB — *Grizzly hackle with barbs slightly shorter than the hook gape, or trimmed short*
WING — *Sparse woodduck flank over which are matched sections of natural goose or mallard wing quill, tied tent shape on top*
HACKLE — *Dark ginger*

HENRYVILLE SPECIAL

HOOK — *Standard length dry fly; sizes 12 to 18*
THREAD — *Olive*
BODY — *Olive fur dubbing*
HACKLE — *Grizzly, 4 to 5 turns at the center of the body, clipped in a "V" at the bottom*
UNDERWING — *Sparse elk hair*
WING — *Two dun-color hen back feather tips, reinforced with a drop of vinyl cement applied at the base of each feather*
ANTENNAE — *Stems of the wing feathers, stripped*
COMMENT — *This slow water style can be tied in any color variation you want.*

SLOW WATER CADDIS

HOOK — *Standard length dry fly; sizes 12 to 18*
THREAD — *Olive*
TAIL — *Gold Z-lon*
BODY — *Olive Antron dubbing*
WING — *Natural mule deer body hair*
HEAD — *Butt ends of the wing, clipped short*
COMMENT — *The tail on this fly represents the trailing pupal shuck of a newly emerged caddisfly.*

X CADDIS

WET FLIES

BLUE DUN

HOOK — *Standard length wet fly; sizes 8 to 14*
THREAD — *Gray*
TAIL — *Medium blue dun hackle barbs*
BODY — *Gray dubbing or spun fur*
HACKLE — *Medium blue dun*
WING — *Gray duck wing quill segments*
COMMENT — *An old standard wet fly.*

GRAY HACKLE

HOOK — *Standard length wet fly; sizes 8 to 16*
THREAD — *Black*
TAIL — *Red hackle barbs (optional)*
BODY — *Peacock herl*
WING — *None*
HACKLE — *Grizzly*
COMMENT — *A simple yet effective wet fly. A similar fly, the
Brown Hackle, is identical except brown hackle
replaces the grizzly.*

**IRON BLUE
WINGLESS**

HOOK — *Standard length wet fly; sizes 12 to 18*
THREAD — *Red*
TAIL — *Honey dun hackle barbs*
BODY — *Mole fur or dark muskrat dubbed onto red thread. At
rear of body, leave some of red thread showing*
HACKLE — *Honey dun, preferably with brownish outside
edges, collar slightly tied back*
COMMENT — *A Jim Leisenring pattern which is very effective.*

**LEADWING
COACHMAN**

HOOK — *Standard length wet fly; sizes 10 to 16*
THREAD — *Black*
TAG — *Flat gold tinsel*
BODY — *Peacock herl*
HACKLE — *Coachman brown*
WING — *Dark gray duck wing quill segments*

PARMACHENE BELLE

HOOK — *Standard length wet fly; sizes 8 to 14*
THREAD — *Black*
TAIL — *Mixed red and white hackle barbs*
BODY — *Yellow floss*
RIB — *Flat gold tinsel*
WING — *Married sections of red and white duck wing quills,
red on top*
HACKLE — *Mixed red and white*
COMMENT — *Still a popular and colorful attractor fly.*

HOOK — *Standard length wet fly; sizes 10 to 16*
THREAD — *Orange*
TAIL — *None*
BODY — *Rear 2/3rd orange floss, front 1/3rd mixed black and brown hare's mask dubbing*
HACKLE — *Brown partridge*
COMMENT — *This is an example of the "soft-hackled" style fly recommended by many anglers. Also popular with green or yellow body, matching thread, and brown or gray partridge hackle.*

PARTRIDGE & ORANGE

HOOK — *Standard length wet fly; sizes 8 to 14*
THREAD — *Black*
TAIL — *Red hackle barbs or red duck quill segment*
BODY — *Yellow floss*
RIB — *Flat gold tinsel*
HACKLE — *Brown*
WING — *Mallard flank*

PROFESSOR

HOOK — *Standard length wet fly; sizes 12 to 18*
THREAD — *Olive*
TAIL — *Woodduck flank barbs*
BODY — *Stripped peacock quill*
RIB — *Fine gold wire*
WING — *Woodduck flank*
HACKLE — *Dark blue dun*

QUILL GORDON

HOOK — *Standard length wet fly; sizes 6 to 18*
THREAD — *Black*
TAG — *Flat gold tinsel*
REAR HACKLE — *Brown*
BODY — *Peacock herl reinforced by overwrap of fine gold wire*
FRONT HACKLE — *White*
COMMENT — *An extremely popular Rocky Mountains pattern, often tied as a dry fly; also often weighted.*

RENEGADE

HOOK — *Wet fly, 2X to 4X long; sizes 4 to 12*
THREAD — *Black*
TAIL — *Short red wool*
BODY — *Black chenille*
RIB — *Oval silver tinsel (optional)*
HACKLE — *Grizzly saddle hackle palmered over the body*
COMMENT — *Also popular with a red, yellow, olive, or brown body, with grizzly or brown hackle. Frequently weighted.*

WOOLY WORM

ALL-PURPOSE NYMPHS

CASUAL DRESS

HOOK — *Nymph, 2X or 3X long; sizes 6 to 12*
THREAD — *Black*
TAIL — *Muskrat fur with the guard hairs left in*
BODY — *Muskrat fur using loop dubbing twisted tight to give a segmented effect*
THORAX — *Thick muskrat fur with the guard hairs tied pointing rearward*
HEAD — *Black ostrich herl*

HARE'S EAR (FLASHBACK)

HOOK — *Nymph, 1X or 2X long; sizes 6 to 18*
THREAD — *Brown*
TAIL — *4 or 5 strands woodduck flank*
BODY — *Dubbing mixture of black, brown and gray fur from base of ears of English Hare's mask. Made thick at the thorax*
RIB — *Fine oval gold, tinsel*
WINGCASE — *Clump of pearl Flashabou over thorax*
LEGS — *Fur from thorax is picked out on each side*
COMMENT — *The flashback wingcase can be applied to many different nymphs.*

PRINCE

HOOK — *Nymph, 1X or 2X long; sizes 8 to 14*
THREAD — *Black*
TAIL — *2 dyed brown goose biots*
BODY — *Peacock herl*
RIB — *Oval gold tinsel*
HACKLE — *Soft brown, wound as a collar*
WING — *2 white goose biots*

SERENDIPITY

HOOK — *Curved nymph, 1X short to 1X long; sizes 10 to 22*
THREAD — *Black, or to match body*
BODY — *Twisted Z-lon*
RIB — *Fine wire, optional, color to complement body color*
HEAD — *Natural deer body hair either spun or stacked, forming a head as shown*
COMMENT — *This simple fly has been used to imitate mayflies, midges and caddisflies.*

ZUG BUG

HOOK — *Nymph, 1X or 2X long; sizes 8 to 14*
THREAD — *Black*
TAIL — *3 short strands of peacock sword*
BODY — *Peacock herl tied thick*
RIB — *Oval silver tinsel*
HACKLE — *Soft brown*
WINGCASE — *Mallard breast cut short to extend 1/4th of body length*

HOOK — *Dry fly, standard length or 1X long;*
sizes 12 to 18
THREAD — *Olive*
HEAD — *Brass bead*
TAIL — *Olive hackle barbs*
ABDOMEN — *Olive dubbing*
RIB — *Copper wire*
THORAX — *Olive dubbing*
WINGCASE — *Brown turkey tail segment*
LEGS — *Dark ginger soft hackle, one wrap behind bead*
COMMENT — *Bead heads are added to many nymphs.*

**BEAD HEAD
OLIVE NYMPH**

HOOK — *Dry fly, standard length or 1X short;*
sizes 12 to 18
THREAD — *Black*
TAIL — *Gray Z-lon*
ABDOMEN — *Gray goose biot*
THORAX — *Gray-olive dubbing*
WINGCASE — *Gray CDC*
COMMENT — *Emerging mayflies are sometimes trapped in*
the surface film. This style fly floats at the
surface. Size and color may vary.

CDC EMERGER

HOOK — *Dry or wet fly, standard length or 1X long;*
sizes 8 to 18
THREAD — *Cream*
BODY — *Yellowish brown fur blend*
LEGS — *Light ginger*
WINGCASE — *Brown dyed goose or turkey quill section*
COMMENT — *Also tied in following color combinations:*

Thread	Body	Legs	Wingcase
tan	red/brown	ginger	dark brown
olive	olive/brown	dark ginger	dark gray/brown
brown	dark brown	red/brown	black

**COMPARA-NYMPH
(YELLOW/BROWN)**

HOOK — *Dry fly, standard length to 2X long;*
sizes 10 to 20
THREAD — *Pale yellow*
TAIL — *Pale yellow hackle barbs, tied split*
ABDOMEN — *Cream/yellow fur dubbing*
RIB — *Brown thread*
THORAX — *Same as abdomen*
LEGS — *Very short and sparse pale yellow hackle, clipped top*
and bottom
WINGCASE — *Gray closed-cell foam pulled over the thorax*
COMMENT — *This style can be tied in other colors to*
match various emerging mayflies.

FLOATING NYMPH

HOOK — *Nymph, 1X long; sizes 12 to 20*
THREAD — *Brown*
TAIL — *Ringneck pheasant center tail barbs*
ABDOMEN — *Bunch of ringneck pheasant center tail*
barbs, wrapped
RIB — *Copper wire*
THORAX — *Peacock herl*
WINGCASE — *Ringneck pheasant center tail barbs, folded*
over the thorax
LEGS — *A few barbs from the wingcase, pulled down*
and back

PHEASANT TAIL

**EPHEMERA
(GREEN DRAKE)**

HOOK — *Nymph, 2X or 3X long; sizes 4 to 8*
THREAD — *Brown*
TAIL — *Three tan or tan/gray ostrich herl tips,
1/3 body length*
ABDOMEN — *Light cream/amber seal fur or dubbing
substitute, marked on back with brown waterproof ink
marker; picked out on sides*
THORAX — *Cream/amber fur with guard hairs, loop
dubbed to also form legs*
WINGCASE — *Brown goose quill section*

**EPHEMERELLA
(HENDRICKSON)**

HOOK — *Nymph, 1X or 2X long; sizes 10 and 12*
THREAD — *Brown*
TAIL — *Well marked woodduck flank barbs, 1/2 body length*
ABDOMEN — *Amber/reddish brown dubbing, picked out
lightly on sides*
WINGCASE — *Dark mottled turkey tail section*
THORAX — *Same as abdomen*
LEGS — *Brown partridge or grouse hackle applied as collar
and tied back before wingcase is brought forward*

HEXAGENIA

HOOK — *Nymph or streamer, 4X or 6X long; sizes 6 to 10*
THREAD —*Tan*
TAIL —*Webby brown hen barbs and filoplume*
ABDOMEN — *Pale yellow fur or synthetic dubbing*
GILLS — *Gray filoplume, on length of each side*
BACK — *Brown turkey tail or pheasant tail*
RIB — *Gold wire*
THORAX — *Same as abdomen*
WINGCASE — *Brown turkey tail or pheasant tail*
LEGS — *Brown partridge body feather, under the wingcase*

ISONYCHIA

HOOK — *Nymph, 1X or 2X long; sizes 8 and 10*
THREAD — *Brown*
TAIL — *Three peacock herl tips, 1/3 body length*
ABDOMEN — *Dark purple/brown seal fur or substitute;
also thin white strip of light moose mane tied over abdomen
and wing case. Pick out fur a little on sides to represent gills*
RIB — *Claret thread*
THORAX — *Well marked grayish guard hairs and fur from
a hare's mask, loop dubbed to also form legs*
WINGCASE — *Dark grayish/brown latex, cut to shape,
1/3 body length*

**STENONEMA
(MARCH BROWN)**

HOOK — *Nymph, 1X or 2X long; sizes 10 and 12*
THREAD — *Brown*
TAIL — *3 strands of cock ringneck pheasant tail, spread out*
ABDOMEN — *Dubbed mixture of amber seal fur and tan
fur from a red fox*
RIB — *Brown cotton thread*
WINGCASE — *Mottled gray/brown segment from
underside of a ringneck pheasant tail*
THORAX — *Same as abdomen*
LEGS — *Brown partridge hackle barbs*

BLACK STONE

HOOK — *Nymph, 2X or 3X long; sizes 2 to 8*
THREAD — *Black*
TAIL & ANTENNA — *Brown goose quill barbs*
ABDOMEN — *Weighted with lead wire on each side of hook shank. Wrap with 3/16" wide strip of heavy latex dyed dark gray to dark brown*
THORAX — *Tied in two sections. First 1/2: a rough-loop dubbing of dark brown dyed rabbit fur and guard hairs forming thorax and legs simultaneously. Tie in a wingcase of dark brown heavy latex; cut to shape. Next 1/2 repeat the same process*

BROOK'S MONTANA STONE

HOOK — *Nymph, 3X or 4X long; sizes 4 to 8*
THREAD — *Black*
TAIL — *Six barbs of crow wing or similar*
ABDOMEN — *Black fuzzy yarn*
RIB — *Copper wire*
THORAX — *Same as abdomen, tied thick*
LEGS — *2 wraps each of mixed natural grizzly and dyed brown grizzly*
GILLS — *Gray ostrich herl wrapped next to the grizzly hackles*
COMMENT — *This "round style" gives a uniform silhouette viewed from all sides.*

MONTANA

HOOK — *Nymph, 2X or 3X long; sizes 2 to 12*
THREAD — *Black*
TAIL — *Black goose quill barbs or hackle barbs*
ABDOMEN — *Black chenille*
THORAX — *Yellow chenille*
LEGS — *Black hackle palmered over thorax*
WINGCASE — *Two strands black chenille tied down over top of the thorax*
COMMENT — *A popular stonefly, usually weighted.*

RUBBERLEGS

HOOK — *Nymph, 4X long; sizes 2 to 10*
THREAD — *Black*
UNDERBODY — *Lead wire*
TAIL — *Two strips of black rubber hackle*
LEGS — *Three pairs of black rubber hackles, spaced along the upper part of body, tied in at the thorax area*
BODY — *Black chenille*
ANTENNA — *Two strips of black rubber hackle*
COMMENT — *A similar fly, the Girdle Bug, uses white rubber hackle.*

YELLOW STONE

HOOK — *Nymph, 2X or 3X long; sizes 6 to 12*
THREAD — *Yellow*
TAIL — *Ginger goose quill barbs tied in a "V"*
ABDOMEN — *Weighted. Pale yellow dubbing*
SHELLBACK — *Speckled turkey dyed yellow*
RIB — *Light brown heavy thread*
THORAX — *Same as abdomen*
LEGS — *Gray partridge dyed yellow with stem tied on top of thorax, concave side down*
WINGCASE — *Darkly marked speckled turkey, dyed yellow, pulled over the thorax and legs*

OTHER NYMPHS

CASED CADDIS LARVA

HOOK — *Nymph, 1X to 3X long; sizes 10 to 16*
THREAD — *Black*
UNDERBODY — *Lead wire*
CASE — *Blended black, brown, olive, and amber furs, or any similar blend of materials to resemble the debris that a case-building caddis uses to construct its shelter*
RIB — *Fine oval gold tinsel*
BODY — *Bright green synthetic dubbing*
HEAD — *Dark brown dubbing*
LEGS — *Six to 8 partridge hackle barbs*

DEEP CADDIS PUPA (BROWN & GREEN)

HOOK — *Standard dry fly; sizes 10 to 18*
THREAD — *Black*
UNDERBODY — *Lead wire*
BODY — *Dubbing blend of 2/3 bright green craft fur and 1/3 olive Antron*
OVERBODY — *A sheath of olive-green Antron*
HACKLE — *Few strands of brown partridge tied to extend below the body*
HEAD — *Brown fur*

GRAY/OLIVE SHRIMP

HOOK — *Standard or curved shank wet fly; sizes 8 to 14*
THREAD — *Olive*
TAIL — *Few olive hackle barbs*
BODY — *A blend of gray, tan and olive synthetic dubbing*
SHELLBACK — *Clear strip cut from a heavy polybag*
RIB — *Fine silver or black wire over body and shellback*
LEGS — *Pick out fur on bottom of body*
COMMENT — *Also tied in brown, tan, gray, and olive, to match naturals.*

HOOK — *Nymph or streamer, 3X to 6X long; sizes 6 to 10*
THREAD — *Black*
TAIL — *Black goose biots*
ABDOMEN — *Black floss*
RIB — *Black ostrich herl over abdomen*
WINGCASE — *Black goose quill section pulled over top of completed thorax and legs*
THORAX — *Dubbed black fur under which is strip of red wool*
LEGS — *Black hackle palmered over thorax, plus at head goose quill fibers tied at each side to flare outward*

HELLGRAMMITE

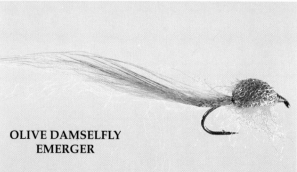

HOOK — *Standard or short shank dry fly; sizes 12 to 14*
THREAD — *Olive*
BODY & TAIL — *A very narrow strip of rabbit fur, dyed olive*
THORAX — *Olive dubbing*
WINGCASE — *Blue closed-cell foam pulled over the thorax*
LEGS — *Fur picked out from the thorax*

OLIVE DAMSELFLY EMERGER

HOOK — *Streamer, 3X or 4X long; sizes 6 to 14*
THREAD — *Black*
TAIL — *Short red wool*
BODY — *Flat silver tinsel*
RIB — *Oval silver tinsel*
WING — *White bucktail, over which is black bucktail, over which is brown bucktail*

BLACK NOSE DACE

HOOK — *Streamer, 4X or 6X long; sizes 6 to 12*
THREAD — *Yellow*
TAG — *Flat gold tinsel*
TAIL — *Two yellow hackle tips*
BODY — *Yellow chenille; keep a slim shape*
THROAT — *Two red hackle tips*
WING — *Small amount of brown portion of a bucktail dyed yellow*
CHEEKS — *Jungle cock (optional)*

DARK EDSON TIGER

HOOK — *Streamer, 4X or 6X long; sizes 4 to 14*
THREAD — *Black*
TAIL — *Red floss over which is small amount of bright green bucktail*
BODY — *Cream spun fur*
RIB — *Flat silver tinsel*
THROAT — *Small bunch of orange bucktail*
WING — *Equal bunches: white bucktail, over which is orange bucktail, over which is bright green bucktail. Over this is an equal size bunch of barred badger (or gray squirrel)*
CHEEKS — *Jungle cock (optional)*

LITTLE BROOK TROUT

HOOK — *Streamer, 4X or 6X long; sizes 4 to 14*
THREAD — *Black*
TAIL — *Small bronze ringneck pheasant breast feather, curving upward*
BODY — *White spun fur*
RIB — *Copper wire or fine flat gold tinsel*
WING — *Equal bunches: yellow bucktail, over which is red/orange bucktail, over which is dark gray squirrel tail, over which is dark red squirrel tail*
CHEEKS — *Jungle cock (optional)*

LITTLE BROWN TROUT

HOOK — *Streamer, 4X or 6X long; sizes 4 to 14*
THREAD — *Black*
TAIL — *Bright green bucktail*
BODY — *Pale pink spun fur*
RIB — *Flat silver tinsel*
THROAT — *Pink bucktail, short*
WING — *Equal bunches: white bucktail, over which is pink bucktail, over which is bright green bucktail, over which is barred badger (or gray squirrel)*
CHEEKS — *Jungle cock (optional)*

LITTLE RAINBOW TROUT

BUCKTAILS

LLAMA

HOOK — *Streamer, 3X or 4X long; sizes 6 to 12*
THREAD — *Black*
TAIL — *Soft grizzly barbs*
BODY — *Red floss or wool*
RIB — *Oval gold tinsel*
WING — *Woodchuck body hair, using both the marked guard hairs and the light colored soft underfur*
HACKLE — *Soft grizzly, collared and slightly tied back*
COMMENT — *A painted white eye with black pupil is optional.*

MICKEY FINN

HOOK — *Streamer, 3X or 4X long; sizes 4 to 14*
THREAD — *Black*
BODY — *Flat silver tinsel*
RIB — *Oval silver tinsel*
WING — *Small bunch of yellow bucktail, over which is an equal size bunch of red bucktail, over which is a larger bunch of yellow bucktail*
COMMENT — *Probably the best known of all trout flies, it is still a very popular attractor pattern.*

RED & WHITE

HOOK — *Streamer, 3X or 4X long; sizes 4 to 14*
THREAD — *Red*
TAIL — *None*
BODY — *Flat silver tinsel*
RIB — *Oval silver tinsel*
WING — *White bucktail, over which is equal amount of red bucktail, over which is peacock herl*
EYES — *Painted white with a black pupil*
COMMENT — *There are several other variations of this pattern.*

**THUNDER CREEK
(SWAMP DARTER)**

HOOK — *Streamer, 3X or 4X long, straight eye; sizes 4 to 12*
THREAD — *White*
BODY — *Silver embossed tinsel, on rear 2/3rd of shank*
WING — *First tie in 2 grizzly hackles extending over the body. Tie brown bucktail on top, with tips extending forward. Now tie white bucktail on bottom, also extending forward. Wrap thread from hook eye back 1/3rd on shank. Fold bucktail toward rear, keeping colors separated, and tie down. Epoxy head and paint gills and eyes*
COMMENT — *Keep it sparse.*

WARDEN'S WORRY

HOOK — *Streamer, 3X or 4X long; sizes 6 to 12*
THREAD — *Black*
TAG — *Flat gold tinsel*
TAIL — *Narrow section of red duck quill*
BODY — *Orange/yellow loose wool or dubbing*
RIB — *Oval gold tinsel*
THROAT — *Yellow hackle collar, tied down*
WING — *Light brown bucktail*

HOOK — *Streamer, 3X or 4X long; sizes 4 to 10*
THREAD — *Black*
BODY — *Cream/yellow synthetic yarn or dubbing with a small amount of red dubbing at the throat*
RIB — *Fine oval gold tinsel*
WING — *4 badger hackles tied in at front. Raise and separate the hackle fibers on top of body and carefully wind the tinsel rib through the separations, binding down the hackles*
HACKLE — *Badger hackle, collared and slightly tied back*

BADGER MATUKA

HOOK — *Streamer, 4X or 6X long; sizes 2 to 12*
THREAD — *Black*
TAIL — *Yellow hackle barbs*
BODY — *Black floss or black wool*
RIB — *Flat silver tinsel*
WING — *White saddle hackle*
THROAT — *Yellow hackle barbs, beard style*
CHEEKS — *Jungle cock*

BLACK GHOST

HOOK — *Streamer, 4X to 6X long; sizes 2 to 12*
THREAD — *Black*
BODY — *Golden yellow floss*
RIB — *Flat silver tinsel*
THROAT — *4 or 5 peacock herl strands next to body, then sparse white bucktail, then short golden pheasant crest*
WING — *Underwing: golden pheasant crest full length of body. Overwing: 4 gray saddle hackles*
SHOULDER — *Silver pheasant body feather*
CHEEKS — *Jungle cock*
COMMENT — *New England's best known streamer fly.*

GRAY GHOST

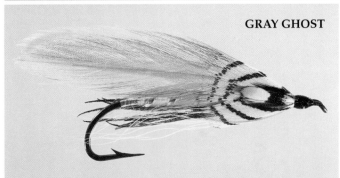

HOOK — *Streamer, 3X or 4X long; sizes 2 to 10*
THREAD — *Brown*
BODY — *Creamy tan fuzzy yarn or dubbing*
RIB — *Heavy oval gold tinsel*
THROAT — *Red yarn or dubbing*
WING & TAIL — *Two or more speckled brown hen back (body) feathers tied down matuka style using the tinsel rib*
HEAD — *Brown lamb's wool stacked over a little white lamb's wool, trimmed to shape*

HENBACK SCULPIN

HOOK — *Nymph, 2X or 3X long; sizes 6 to 16*
THREAD — *Black*
BODY — *Flat silver tinsel*
WING — *Underwing: yellow hair, hackle barbs or hackle tips. Overwing: a mallard flank feather on each side, concave sides cupped together over the body and underwing*
HACKLE — *Grizzly, or brown and grizzly mixed*
EYES — *Jungle cock (optional)*
COMMENT — *A very popular variation has a wing of a folded mallard flank feather, tied flat on top, and no eyes. In small sizes it's often fished as a dry fly.*

HORNBERG SPECIAL

STREAMERS

JOE'S SMELT

HOOK — *Streamer, 4X or 6X long; sizes 2 to 6*
THREAD — *Red*
TAIL — *Short red hackle barbs*
BODY — *Braided mylar tinsel with cotton core removed. Hook shank is inserted through the tinsel which is then tied at the rear and front with red thread, and cemented*
WING — *Pintail flank or long mallard flank, tied flat over the top*
HEAD — *Black with painted yellow eye and black pupil*

KIWI MUDDLER

HOOK — *Streamer, 2X or 3X long; sizes 2 to 10*
UNDERBODY — *Lead wire*
BODY — *Pearlescent mylar tubing, secured at the rear with white thread*
TAIL — *Unravelled pearlescent mylar*
WING — *A diamond-shaped rabbit fur strip, tapering to a point at the rear, over which are a few strands of pearl crystal flash*
HEAD & COLLAR — *Spun natural and olive-dyed deer body hair, trimmed broad, flat on top and bottom*

LIGHT SPRUCE

HOOK — *Streamer, 2X or 3X long; sizes 4 to 10*
THREAD — *Black*
TAIL — *4 peacock sword fibers*
BODY — *Rear 1/3 red floss, front 2/3 peacock herl*
WING — *Two light badger hackles*
COLLAR — *Light badger hackle collared and tied back*
COMMENT — *Also tied as a wet fly for Cutthroat trout. Frequently tied with the wings splayed to each side.*

MUDDLER MINNOW

HOOK — *Streamer, 2X or 3X long; sizes 2 to 14*
THREAD — *Brown*
TAIL — *Section from mottled turkey quill*
BODY — *Gold tinsel wrapped over rear 2/3 of hook shank*
WING — *Underwing of gray squirrel (some use brown calftail), overwing of paired sections of speckled turkey quill, tied on edge*
HEAD — *Spun gray/brown deer body hair, front part clipped to shape, leaving a collar of hair at rear of head*
COMMENT — *Fished wet or dry, weighted or unweighted, and in various colors (yellow, white, black and green), this is one of the best flies around.*

NINE THREE

HOOK — *Streamer, 4X or 6X long; sizes 2 to 12*
THREAD — *Black*
BODY — *Flat silver tinsel*
WING — *Underwing: a small bunch of white bucktail. Overwing: 2 green saddle hackles flanked by 2 black saddle hackles*
CHEEKS — *Jungle cock*
COMMENT — *Originally, the fly had green saddle tied flat over shank with the black saddle tied above, on edge.*

HOOK — *Streamer, 3X or 4X long; sizes 2 to 10*
THREAD — *Brown*
TAIL — *Short bunch brown calftail*
BODY — *Rear 3/4 cream dubbed fur, next 1/4 red fur. Total body is 3/4 of hook shank*
WING — *Tie in small bunch of brown calftail, extending body length. Then, tie in 4 grizzly hackles, dyed brown. Add a small bunch of short red squirrel on each side*
COLLAR — *Brown antelope hair with tips toward rear*
HEAD — *Brown antelope hair spun on and clipped short top and bottom. Sides clipped to overall bullet shape as viewed from top*

SPUDDLER

HOOK — *Streamer, 4X or 6X long; sizes 2 to 12*
THREAD — *Black*
TAIL — *Short thin red wool*
BODY — *Flat silver tinsel*
RIB — *Oval silver tinsel*
WING — *Underwing: sparse bunch of white bucktail. Overwing: 4 light blue saddle hackles*
SHOULDER — *Pale green hackles, 2/3rd length of wing, one on each side*
CHEEKS — *Jungle cock*
TOPPING — *4 or 5 strands of peacock herl*

SUPERVISOR

HOOK — *Streamer, 2X or 3X long; sizes 2 to 12*
THREAD — *White*
TAIL — *Red hackle barbs*
BODY — *Silver tinsel chenille*
WING — *Underwing: small bunch of gray or red squirrel over which is longer white marabou. Top with 4 or 5 strands of peacock herl*
HEAD — *Gray/brown deer body hair tied same as on the Muddler Minnow*
COMMENT — *Often weighted, also popular in black, gray, brown, olive, and yellow.*

WHITE MARABOU MUDDLER

HOOK — *Streamer, 2X or 3X long; sizes 2 to 14*
THREAD — *Black (or to match body)*
UNDERBODY — *Lead wire (optional)*
TAIL — *Black marabou*
BODY — *Purple chenille*
HACKLE — *Black, the tip tied in at the rear, palmered over the body with a few extra turns at the front*
RIB — *Gold wire*
COMMENT — *This pattern, in different colors and variations, has recently evolved as a favorite of many top fishermen.*

WOOLLY BUGGER

HOOK — *Streamer, 3X or 4X long; sizes 2 to 8*
THREAD — *Black and yellow*
UNDERBODY — *Lead or aluminum tape, folded over and trimmed to a minnow shape*
BODY — *Silver or pearl mylar tubing*
THROAT — *Yellow hackle*
WING — *Rabbit fur strip secured at the head, pulled back over the body and tied down with yellow thread*
COMMENT — *Originally tied with the hook point down, this is often tied on a straight eye hook with the point inverted.*

ZONKER

BLACK FLYING ANT

HOOK — *Standard dry fly; sizes 10 to 20*
THREAD — *Black*
BODY — *Tie in two distinct segments using black dubbed fur. The abdomen is slightly larger than the head*
LEGS — *Before tying head, wrap 1 or 2 turns of black hackle*
WINGS — *Before tying head, apply 2 light blue dun hackle points splayed one to each side, down wing style*
COMMENT — *Can also be tied with synthetic Z-lon wings, or as a wet fly using lacquered black thread for the body.*

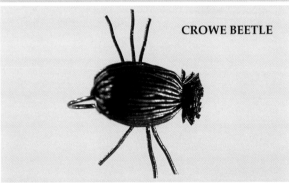

CROWE BEETLE

HOOK — *Standard dry fly; sizes 10 to 18*
THREAD — *Black*
BODY — *Black thread wrapped over black deer body hair. Dubbing may be applied to the body for a wider silhouette*
SHELLBACK — *Black deer body hair over top of body. Coat with vinyl cement*
LEGS — *Three black hairs from the shellback, pulled out on each side*
HEAD — *Balance of deer hair cut short over the eye of the hook*

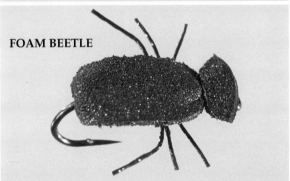

FOAM BEETLE

HOOK — *Standard dry fly; sizes 12 to 22*
THREAD — *Olive*
BODY — *None, tying thread only*
LEGS — *Beetle legs, or substitute, three pairs*
BACK — *Strip of olive closed-cell foam*
HEAD — *Foam from the back, trimmed short*
COMMENT — *Many fishermen like to paint a bright fluorescent dot on top of the back so they can see the fly more easily.*

INCHWORM

HOOK — *Standard dry fly, 1X or 2X long; sizes 12 and 14*
THREAD — *Insect green*
BODY — *Wrap the hook shank with tying thread, leaving thread at rear. Take a long bunch (20-24 strands) of deer body hair dyed insect green and lay it parallel to top of hook so the middle of the bunch is above the hook eye. Wrap the thread forward in well-spaced turns. Fold back the deer hair, thus making a double bunch, and loosely wrap full length, even beyond hook bend, and return the thread to the head and tie off. Coat the finished fly with vinyl cement*

RED FLYING ANT

HOOK — *Standard dry fly; sizes 12 to 20*
THREAD — *Black*
ABDOMEN — *Red fur*
OUTRIGGERS — *Black moose or elk hair, one on each side*
WING — *Section of gray duck wing quill tied flat on top over the abdomen, coated with vinyl cement*
LEGS — *Dark dun hackle*
THORAX — *Red fur*

HOOK — *Dry fly, 2X long; sizes 6 to 14*
THREAD — *Tan*
TAIL — *Red hackle barbs*
BODY — *Pale yellow acrylic wool or polypropylene. Extend body by first placing loop of wool over tail, then wind body*
RIB — *Brown hackle. After wrapping, trim hackle short*
WING — *Yellow deer body hair over which is a tent wing of mottled turkey wing quill segment*
LEGS — *Trimmed grizzly hackle stems, dyed yellow*
HEAD & COLLAR — *Natural brown deer body hair dyed yellow, spun and trimmed as shown*

DAVE'S HOPPER

HOOK — *Dry fly, 1X or 2X long; sizes 8 to 16*
THREAD — *Yellow*
BODY — *Yellow, round closed cell foam, slit lengthwise and secured over the hook shank*
WING — *A clump of natural deer body hair, dyed yellow, the tips extending rearward past bend of hook*
LEGS — *Yellow round rubber tied on each side*
COMMENT — *Also tied in tan, green and orange.*

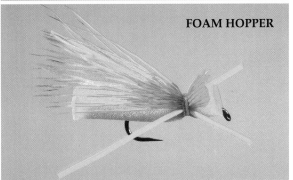
FOAM HOPPER

HOOK — *Dry fly, 1X or 2X long; sizes 8 to 14*
THREAD — *Black*
BODY — *Dubbed black fur*
WING — *Section from black goose quill tied flat over body*
OVERWING — *Tie on top a clump of black deer body hair, the tips extending rearward past bend of hook*
HEAD — *Black deer body hair clipped fairly short*
COMMENT — *The Letort Hopper is tied in the same style but features a yellow body, oak turkey wing and natural deer body hair.*

LETORT CRICKET

HOOK — *Wet fly, 1X or 2X long; sizes 4 to 10*
THREAD — *Brown*
CLAWS — *Two bunches of red squirrel tail hair, splayed to each side*
BODY — *Brown or olive wool*
RIB — *Brown hackle palmered over body and pulled down*
SHELLBACK — *Section from brown goose or turkey wing quill, well lacquered once fly is completed*
COMMENT — *Color depends on geography and time of year. Fly is tied in reverse to imitate the crayfish's backward swimming motion.*

CRAYFISH

HOOK — *Wet fly, 2X or 3X long, or keel hook; sizes 4 to 10*
THREAD — *Claret*
TAIL — *Thick clump of claret marabou*
BODY — *Claret mohair or similar, tied to be thick at rear, tapering forward*
HACKLE — *Very sparse soft claret hackle, collared*
COMMENT — *Often weighted; tied in black, gray, olive, and various shades of brown.*

LEECH

BRINDLE BUG

HOOK — *Salmon/steelhead wet fly, or streamer, 2X or 3X long; sizes 2 to 10*
THREAD — *Black*
TAG — *Fine oval gold tinsel*
TAIL — *Two divided brown hackle tips*
BODY — *Black and yellow variegated or mixed chenille (the first turn of chenille is made under the tail to cock it upward)*
RIB — *Fine oval gold tinsel (optional)*
COLLAR — *Brown hackle*
COMMENT — *This fly is frequently weighted.*

BURLAP

HOOK — *Salmon/steelhead wet fly, or streamer, 2X or 3X long; sizes 2 to 10*
THREAD — *Black*
TAG — *Fine oval gold tinsel*
TAIL — *Natural deer body hair, tied full*
BODY — *Burlap fiber tied full and roughened to look shaggy*
COLLAR — *Soft grizzly, slightly oversize*

COMET

HOOK — *Various salmon/steelhead or wet fly, standard length to 3X long; sizes 2 to 10*
THREAD — *Fluorescent orange*
TAG — *Fine oval gold tinsel*
TAIL — *Long orange hair or hackle barbs*
BODY — *Oval or flat silver tinsel*
COLLAR — *Orange hackle or schlappen*
EYES — *Gold or silver bead chain*
COMMENT — *The Comet is a fly style rather than a specific pattern. It is tied in many colors and with varying materials.*

EGG SUCKING LEECH (LEAD EYE)

HOOK — *Streamer, 3X or 4X long; sizes 2 to 8*
THREAD — *To match head*
TAIL — *Black rabbit fur strip*
BODY — *Black chenille*
RIB — *Fine silver wire*
HACKLE — *Soft black, hackle tied in by the tip and palmered over body*
HEAD — *A ball (egg) of fluorescent chenille, usually red, orange, pink or green, tied around chrome lead dumbbell eyes*

GREASE LINER

HOOK — *Salmon dry or 2X long dry fly; sizes 2 to 10*
THREAD — *Black*
TAIL — *Fine brown deer body hair*
BODY — *Dark rusty tan to black dubbed fur*
THROAT — *A sparse beard of grizzly hackle*
WING — *Dark deer body hair extending only to the end of the dubbing, clipped to form a head from the butt ends*

HOOK — *Salmon/steelhead wet fly; sizes 2 to 10*
THREAD — *Black*
TAIL — *Red hackle barbs*
BODY — *Orange or fluorescent orange chenille*
COLLAR — *Orange hackle*
WING — *Natural polar bear or white bucktail*

POLAR SHRIMP

HOOK — *Salmon/steelhead wet fly, or streamer, 3X or 4X long; sizes 3/0 to 2*
THREAD — *Fluorescent red*
WING 1 — *Tied about 2/3 way up the hook shank: Orange marabou around which is gold and purple Flashabou*
WING 2 — *Fluorescent red marabou*
COLLAR — *Purple schlappen hackle*

POPSICLE

HOOK — *Salmon/steelhead wet fly; sizes 2 to 10*
THREAD — *Black*
TAG — *Flat silver tinsel*
TAIL — *Long red hackle barbs (or purple)*
BODY — *Purple wool or chenille*
RIB — *Oval silver tinsel*
WING — *Brown bucktail*
COLLAR — *Purple hackle*

PURPLE PERIL

HOOK — *Salmon/steelhead wet fly; sizes 2 to 10*
THREAD — *Black*
TAG — *Flat silver tinsel*
TAIL — *Mallard flank feather barbs or red hackle barbs*
BODY — *Black chenille*
RIB — *Flat or oval silver tinsel*
WING — *A pair of grizzly hackle tips curving away from each other*
COLLAR — *Soft grizzly hackle*

SILVER HILTON

HOOK — *Salmon/steelhead wet fly; sizes 2 to 10*
THREAD — *Black*
TAIL — *Red hackle barbs*
BUTT — *Fluorescent green chenille*
BODY — *Black chenille or wool*
RIB — *Flat or oval silver tinsel*
COLLAR — *Black hackle*
WING — *White skunk hair or substitute*
COMMENT — *This is arguably the best known of all steelhead flies. It is tied in many variations.*

**SKUNK
(GREEN BUTT)**

BLACK BEAR, GREEN BUTT

HOOK — *Salmon wet fly; sizes 1/0 to 12*
THREAD — *Black*
TAG — *Oval silver tinsel*
TIP — *Fluorescent green wool or floss*
TAIL — *Golden pheasant crest (optional)*
BODY — *Black floss or wool*
RIB — *Oval silver tinsel*
THROAT — *Black hackle collared and tied down*
WING — *Black bear hair or black squirrel tail*

BLUE CHARM (HAIRWING)

HOOK — *Salmon wet fly; sizes 2 to 12*
THREAD — *Black*
TAG — *Oval silver tinsel*
TIP — *Golden yellow floss*
BUTT — *Black ostrich herl (optional)*
BODY — *Black floss*
RIB — *Oval silver tinsel*
THROAT — *Teal blue hackle collared and tied down*
WING — *Red squirrel tail*

BOMBER

HOOK — *Salmon wet fly, or streamer 3X or 4X long; sizes 2 to 8*
THREAD — *Brown*
TAIL — *Brown bucktail*
BUTT — *Fluorescent green dubbing (optional)*
WING — *Brown bucktail projecting forward at a 45° angle over the eye of the hook*
BODY — *Natural deer body hair spun tightly and clipped into a cigar shape*
HACKLE — *One or two brown saddle hackles tied in at the butt of the fly and palmered forward*

COSSEBOOM

HOOK — *Salmon wet fly; sizes 1/0 to 10*
THREAD — *Fluorescent red*
TAG — *Embossed or oval silver tinsel*
TAIL — *Light olive floss*
BODY — *Light olive floss*
RIB — *Embossed silver tinsel*
WING — *Gray squirrel tail*
CHEEKS — *Jungle cock (usually omitted)*
HACKLE — *Lemon yellow hackle, collared and tied back*

GREEN HIGHLANDER (HAIRWING)

HOOK — *Salmon wet fly; sizes 1/0 to 8*
TAG — *Flat silver tinsel and pale yellow floss*
TAIL — *Golden pheasant crest*
BUTT — *Black ostrich herl*
BODY — *Rear 1/3 yellow floss; front 2/3 bright grass-green seal or substitute*
RIB — *Oval silver tinsel over entire body; also bright grass-green hackle palmered over front 2/3 of the body*
WING — *Underwing of strands of golden pheasant tippet, over which sparse mixed orange and green soft badger underfur, over which sparse pine squirrel tail*
CHEEKS — *Ringneck pheasant neck feathers, dyed red*
HACKLE — *Bright yellow, collared and tied down*

HOOK — *Salmon wet fly; sizes 1/0 to 8*
TAG — *Silver tinsel and yellow floss*
TAIL — *Golden pheasant crest, red/orange hackle barbs over*
BUTT & JOINT — *Black ostrich herl*
BODY — *Rear half: Golden yellow floss. Front half: Black floss palmered with black hackle*
RIB — *Fine oval silver tinsel and wire*
THROAT — *Guinea fowl*
WING — *Golden pheasant tippets, over which is yellow, red and blue badger underfur, over which is pine squirrel tail*
CHEEKS — *Kingfisher blue feather*

JOCK SCOTT (HAIRWING)

HOOK — *Salmon wet fly; sizes 1/0 to 10*
THREAD — *Red*
TAG — *Oval gold tinsel*
TAIL — *A bunch of peacock sword fibers*
BODY — *Rear half: Orange floss, veiled on top with the same floss extending to the middle of the tail. Front half: Peacock herl*
RIB — *Fine oval gold tinsel*
WING — *Gray fox guard hairs*
COLLAR — *Soft grizzly hackle*
CHEEKS — *Jungle cock (usually omitted)*

RUSTY RAT

HOOK — *Salmon wet fly; sizes 1/0 to 10*
THREAD — *Red*
TAG — *Oval gold tinsel*
TAIL — *Golden pheasant crest*
BODY — *Flat silver tinsel*
RIB — *Fine oval gold tinsel*
WING — *Gray fox guard hairs*
COLLAR — *Soft grizzly hackle*
CHEEKS — *Jungle cock (usually omitted)*

SILVER RAT

HOOK — *Salmon wet fly; sizes 1/0 to 10*
THREAD — *Black*
TAG — *Fine oval gold tinsel, fluorescent green floss and fluorescent red floss*
BODY — *Peacock herl*
RIB — *Fine oval gold tinsel*
THROAT — *Black hackle*
WING — *Black bear hair*
CHEEKS — *Jungle cock (optional)*

UNDERTAKER

HOOK — *Salmon dry fly; sizes 4 to 10*
THREAD — *White*
TAIL — *White bucktail or calftail*
BODY — *Light cream colored dubbing*
WING — *White bucktail or calftail*
HACKLE — *Light colored badger, tied full and bushy*
COMMENT — *The Gray Wulff and Royal Wulff are also popular for Atlantic salmon fishing.*

WHITE WULFF

BASS FLIES

CLOUSER DEEP MINNOW (GOLDEN SHINER)

HOOK — *Streamer or wet fly, standard length to 3X long, straight eye; sizes 2 to 10*
THREAD — *Brown*
EYES — *Lead dumbbell eyes, red with black pupils*
THROAT — *White bucktail*
WING — *Gold crystal flash over which is golden olive bucktail*
COMMENT — *Because the fly rides upside down it's less likely to snag weeds. Tie the Clouser Deep Minnow style in various colors.*

DAHLBERG DIVER

HOOK — *Wet fly, straight eye; sizes 1/0 to 8*
TAIL — *Light olive rabbit fur strip and a few strands of light green Flashabou*
COLLAR & HEAD — *Light olive deer body hair, spun and clipped to shape and cemented on bottom*
COMMENT — *When fished, this fly alternately floats and dives. Marabou and other materials are also used for the tail. The weedguard is optional.*

FUR LEECH

HOOK — *Wet fly, straight eye, wide gape; sizes 1/0 to 8*
THREAD — *Fluorescent green*
TAIL — *Chartreuse rabbit fur strip*
BODY — *Chartreuse cross-cut rabbit fur strip, wrapped over the full length of the hook shank*
EYES — *Silver bead chain or chrome lead eyes with painted black pupils (optional)*
COMMENT — *Is this fly fishing's answer to the plastic worm?*

HAIRBUG

HOOK — *Wet fly, straight eye, wide gape; sizes 1/0 to 8*
WEED GUARD — *Optional*
THREAD — *Red*
TAIL — *White marabou over which is red marabou; two white hackles splayed out on each side*
SKIRT — *White hackle*
BODY — *Bands of red, white and black deer body hair*
LEGS — *Red, white and black rubber hackle*

LEFTY'S BUG

HOOK — *Kinked shank popper hook, straight eye; sizes 2 to 8*
TAIL — *Red or gray squirrel tail*
BODY — *Tapered cork or balsa wood cylinder, cut flat on bottom with a flat face, angled back and painted bright yellow or fluorescent orange with prominent eyes*
COMMENT — *Be sure to maintain the position and proportion of the materials as shown.*

HOOK — *Straight eye, wide gape; sizes 2 to 6*
TAIL — *Chamois strip*
BODY — *Natural dark deer body hair on top (with only the tips of the hair showing and pointing to the rear), stacked over very light gray or natural white deer body hair, trimmed close and flat across the bottom and left entirely untrimmed on top*
EARS — *Brown chamois, tied in front of the body*
HEAD — *Brown dyed deer body hair stacked over natural light gray or white deer body hair, trimmed*
WHISKERS — *Black moose mane or similar, tied back*
EYES — *Solid black beads, or painted*

MOUSERAT

HOOK — *Wet fly, 2X or 3X long; sizes 2 to 8*
UNDERBODY — *Lead wire*
TAIL — *Black ostrich herl*
BODY — *Black chenille*
HACKLE — *Very soft dark dun, palmered over the body*
FEELERS — *Black rubber hackle*

MURRAY'S HELLGRAMMITE

HOOK — *Straight eye, wide gape; sizes 4 to 10*
BUTT — *Yellow deer body hair, spun and trimmed*
LEGS — *Grey rubber hackle, knotted and separated into toes*
UNDERBODY — *Closed cell foam, built up for bulk*
BODY — *Light yellow chenille*
HEAD — *Green deer body hair, spun and trimmed flat on the top and bottom leaving some of the longer strands on the sides to represent front legs*
EYES — *Hollow plastic*

SANG FLOATING FROG

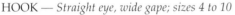

HOOK — *Straight eye, 2X long; sizes 1/0 to 8*
BODY — *Silver gray Antron over the rear 2/3 of the hook*
SKIRT — *Fluorescent gray marabou veiling the body, with pearl and silver crystal flash on each side and peacock herl over the top*
GILLS — *Fluff from the base of a dyed red hackle*
SIDES — *A pair of natural gray mallard flank feathers on each side, slightly shorter than the marabou*
HEAD — *Dyed pearl gray wool, spun around eyes and trimmed as shown*
EYES — *Lead dumbbell, white with black pupils*
COMMENT — *A floating version uses deer body hair for the head, and hollow plastic eyes.*

SHINEABOU SHAD

HOOK — *Silver streamer, 3X or 4X long; sizes 2 to 10*
THROAT — *A ball of fluorescent red yarn or dubbing over which is pearl crystal flash and white Fishair*
WING — *Pearlescent and pearl blue crystal flash, over which is very pale gray lamb's wool and silver Flashabou*
SIDES — *On each side a strip of pearlescent mylar, trimmed to a point, outside of which is a single pale dun-colored badger hackle*
CHEEKS — *Mallard breast feather, curving out*
EYES — *Solid plastic, cemented to the cheeks*

WHITLOCK SHEEP SHAD

SALTWATER FLIES

CLOUSER DEEP ULTRA MINNOW

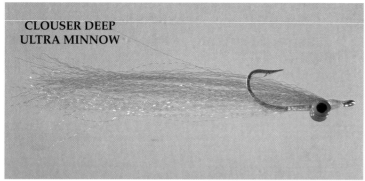

HOOK — *Saltwater, straight eye, standard length; sizes 3/0 to 8*
THREAD — *White*
EYES — *Lead dumbbell eyes secured on top of hook shank, painted red with black pupils*
THROAT — *Polar bear (translucent white/cream) Ultra Hair*
WING — *Green Ultra Hair, over which is a long and short bunch of pearl crystal flash, topped by light blue Ultra Hair*

CRAZY CHARLIE

HOOK — *Saltwater, straight eye, standard length; sizes 4 to 10*
THREAD — *White*
EYES — *Silver bead chain*
TAIL — *Silver Flashabou (optional)*
BODY — *Silver tinsel or Flashabou, overwrapped with clear monofilament or plastic*
WING — *Two white hackle tips or white hair*
COMMENT — *Because of the enormous success of this fly it is now tied in various colors, with many different materials.*

EPOXY SURF CANDY

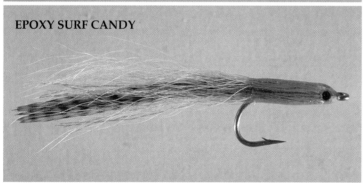

HOOK — *Saltwater, straight eye, standard length; sizes 2/0 to 6*
THREAD — *Color to match wing*
UNDERBODY — *Silver mylar tubing, wrapped (optional)*
WING — *Tied in at head, 4 long dyed grizzly saddle hackles, on each side a few strands of crystal flash, dyed bucktail over, all colors of your choice*
THROAT — *Bucktail, same length as the wing*
HEAD — *An epoxy coating over the front 1/3 of the fly*
EYES — *Peel-off, stick-on prismatic eyes, epoxy coated*

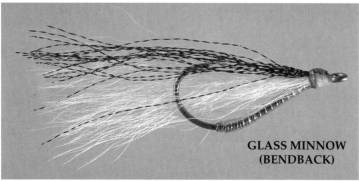

GLASS MINNOW (BENDBACK)

HOOK — *Saltwater, straight eye, 2X or 3X long shank, bent as shown; sizes 2/0 to 8*
THREAD — *White*
BODY — *Flat silver tinsel overwrapped with clear monofilament, or clear plastic*
WING — *White bucktail or substitute, over which is blue crystal flash (optionally blue or green bucktail on top)*
HEAD — *Yellow painted eyes with black pupils (optional)*
GILLS — *Red, thread wraps or painted on*

LEFTY'S DECEIVER

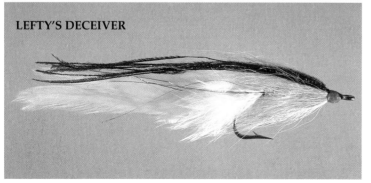

HOOK — *Saltwater, straight eye, standard length; sizes 5/0 to 6*
THREAD — *White, or color of choice*
WING — *Six to ten matched white saddle hackles, outside of which, on each side, a few strands of pearl crystal flash or Flashabou*
BODY — *Same as thread or wrapped oval silver tinsel*
COLLAR — *Two bunches of white bucktail, one applied on each side, extending as shown*
THROAT — *Short red crystal flash(optional)*
TOPPING — *Peacock herl*
COMMENT — *The Deceiver style, in many variations, may be the most used baitfish imitation for saltwater fly fishing.*

HOOK — *Saltwater, straight eye, standard length or long shank; sizes 1/0 to 4*
THREAD — *White*
WING & BODY — *Tied in at the head: white bucktail or synthetic hair, over which is pearl crystal flash and peacock herl, lightly secured with thread for the length of the hook shank*
HEAD — *An epoxy coating over the front 1/3 of the fly*
EYES — *Painted or peel-off, stick-on prismatic eyes*
COMMENT — *The epoxy may contain glitter flakes.*

SAND EEL

HOOK — *Saltwater, straight eye, standard length; sizes 2 to 8*
THREAD — *Black*
BUTT — *Orange yarn or chenille*
BODY — *Tan dubbing or chenille*
WING — *Brown craft fur over pearl crystal flash*

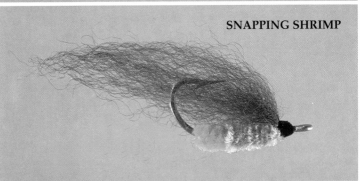

SNAPPING SHRIMP

HOOK — *Saltwater, straight eye, standard length; sizes 4/0 to 4*
THREAD — *White*
WING — *White bucktail over which is green bucktail and pearl Flashabou, over which is blue bucktail, over which is peacock herl*
EYES — *Glass or lead, yellow with black pupils*
COLLAR — *White deer body hair*
HEAD — *Spun white deer body hair, trimmed flat on the sides as shown.*
COMMENT — *This fly may be tied with either a bucktail or marabou wing, using the colors that match the baitfish you want to imitate. The flat shape is critical to the performance of this fly.*

TABORY SLAB SIDE

HOOK — *Saltwater, straight eye, standard length; sizes 4/0 to 4*
THREAD — *Red*
WING — *Long bunch of silver mylar tinsel or Flashabou, surrounded by shorter white bucktail and rainbow crystal flash, a grizzly hackle on each side*
BODY — *Heavy red chenille, about two turns directly in front of the wing*
COLLAR — *Webby white hackle, tied full*
EYES — *Silver bead chain*

WHISTLER (FLASHTAIL)

HOOK — *Saltwater, straight eye, standard length; sizes 2 to 8*
THREAD — *Fluorescent green*
BODY — *Tan fleece or Glo Bug yarn*
EYES — *Melted monofilament, or stamen eyes, painted fluorescent green with black pupils*
LEGS — *Tan rubber hackle, knotted, curving up*
CLAWS — *Two clumps of short tan marabou, and a cree hackle*
BELLY — *Epoxy paste underneath, securing all parts, painted white*

WOOL CRAB

INDEX OF FLY PATTERNS